TOMORROW

YOU

MARRY

47579

by

Joe W. Burton

Illustrated by

Sidney Quinn, Jr.

Broadman Press
Nashville, Tennessee

Printed in the United States of America
12.5S503

ACKNOWLEDGMENTS

We are grateful to the following publishers for permission to quote from their copyrighted materials:

Metropolitan Life Insurance Company, *Statistical Bulletin.*

Houghton Mifflin Company, *Marriage and the Family,* Meyer F. Nimkoff.

Prentice-Hall, Inc., *The Marriage Handbook,* Judson T. Landis and Mary G. Landis.

Parents' Magazine.

Concordia Publishing House.

The Macmillan Company, *Modern Marriage,* Paul Popenoe.

The outline in chapter II summarizing the Christian teachings on marriage is used with the kind permission of Dr. Olin T. Binkley.

CONTENTS

I. Most People Do... 1

II. What Marriage Means................................... 20

III. When You Are of Age................................. 37

IV. Signposts to Success.................................... 56

V. Two Hearts As One..................................... 76

VI. How to Go About It.................................... 94

VII. When Two Strike Out Together................ 111

VIII. Christ's Way in Your Home....................... 131

FIGURES

1. Marriage Rates: United States, 1867—1948........ 5

2. Percentage Who Marry... 8

3. Your Chances of Marriage.................................... 12

4. How Old Are You?... 40

5. Marriages Within Year.. 42

6. Marriage Under Pressure...................................... 48

7. Product of a Happy Home..................................... 58

8. Catholic-Baptist Marriage Is Most Hazardous.... 62

9. Five False Planks in Bogus Romance Platform.. 84

10. Steps to Emotional Maturity.............................. 90

11. Percentage of Population Single, 1940............... 101

12. Ratio of Females to Males.................................... 103

13. Division of Labor in Home.................................... 115

14. A Family Budget.. 119

15. Family Religion 129

Chapter I

Most People Do

And the Lord God said, It is not good that the man should be alone; I will make him an help meet for him.—Genesis 2:18.

And Jesus answering said unto them, The children of this world marry, and are given in marriage.—Luke 20:34.

This is a book about you and one of the most important decisions of your life.

I. Youth's Great Decisions

Young people face three great questions: One in the realm of faith, Who is God, and what shall be my relation to him? One in the area of vocation, What shall I do with my life? The third in the field of social relations, With whom shall I link my life for all of the days and years ahead?

1. *Becoming a Christian*

It is a momentous day when one comes to a decision for Christ. Previously one has gone his own way; life has been lived selfishly according to his own bent and in his own puny strength. But now life is different through personal commitment to Christ. "As for me," says the Christian, "my life is rooted in Christ. I believe that he is the Son of God, that he died for me, and that he rose again victor even for me over death, sin, and hell itself. I live by faith in Christ."

That is a great decision—the decision of faith in Christ which brings salvation. It is the very greatest decision of life, and it is one which is reached most often in the early years.

2. *Choosing a Vocation*

The first great decision of life has to do with quality of living in time and eternity. The second concerns function in the days of man's life on earth. Truly one has passed a second great milestone when he decides upon vocation.

In anticipation of life's work one is challenged by many possibilities. There are over 25,000 classified vocations engaging the activities of the citizens of the United States, according to the United States Department of Commerce. There are many great fields to any one of which a young person may give his life and within each of which one will discover multiplied specific vocations. There is the fundamental task of tilling the soil in the fields of agriculture, ranching, horticulture. Again there is the great vocational area of gathering nature's harvests, including fishing, mining, lumbering. Once more, one may consider the field of manufacturing in any one of a thousand different specialties. Or he may direct his energies to some phase of human relations in government, law, teaching, or social service. Or his attention may be attracted to construction, to a ministry of healing, or to some sales service. Or he may be called to the highest ministry of all and give himself to labor among men on the plane of their relations with God.

Whatever the large area which challenges your interest, and whatever the specific task which you may take up as your vocation, the point noted here is that this is a great decision of life and that it is made in youth. One needs a vast amount of knowledge concerning the beckoning vocational opportunities about him, a keen insight into his own aptitudes, plus an objective and realistic appraisal of the practical possibilities for his own development if he is to make a wise vocational choice. Indeed one needs definite divine guidance in such a decision. He needs proper grounding in faith on the basis of the correct first decision if he is to make the proper second decision.

3. *Picking a Mate*

The third decision is likewise one of great consequence. It has to do with companionship, with association. It amounts to an actual sharing of one's life with another. Joys, sorrows, triumphs, defeats, health, sickness, good fortune, and disaster are to be met as a team. Heretofore you have lived in your family into which you were born. To your parents you have been a child to be guided toward maturity. To others in the family you have been a "big sister" or a "little brother." But when this third decision is made you will for the first time share your life with an equal, with a comrade, on the basis of mutual respect and affection.

This relation is a result of volitional choice. It is based on deliberate decision. You will elect to enter into it.

One needs remarkable insight into his own personality and character in determining to link his life with another. The decision demands fine judgment of the personal qualities of another. One needs for this very great decision an uncanny foreknowledge of how two personalities will blend together in harmony and contentment.

Yes, any young man needs guidance from God before asking any maid to join him at the marriage altar.

Surely any young woman needs to pray long and consider carefully before saying yes to the importunate wooings of her lover.

One could almost say that for each of these three great decisions the wisdom of the aged is needed—and yet each must be made in the wonderfully exciting days of youth.

4. *Basic Assumptions for Decisions*

Now there is with reference to each of these great decisions a basic assumption. First, we assume the existence of God. Most rational people do. Evidence of the Creator is so manifest in his creation that it is hardly necessary to convince the creature of his existence. In saying that the greatest question of life, therefore, is in the realm of faith, we assume that there is a Supreme Being in whom one may trust. Actually such an assumption is normal to the human heart, for few people need any further proof of God's existence than that which they find in their own spiritual nature and in God's handiwork about them.

Second, we assume that one will pursue some vocation. Work is the normal human experience. Even those who do not require economic returns as a motive for employment must find some central unifying activity as a meaningful occupation of their time. The human spirit cannot happily remain idle. Any normal person will seek a principal activity as a chief function of his life, irrespective of any economic pressure. This viewpoint is assumed when we point out that youth's second great question is, What shall I do with my life?

Third, we also asume that one will marry, that he will live not as a hermit unto himself, but in society, the focal point of his social organization being his own home. This seems to be a valid assumption.

II. It's a Fact: Most People Do

Last year—or any year near the middle of the twentieth century—there were close to two million marriages in the United States. On any warm day in June there will be around seven thousand marriages in this country, and any cool morning in January will usher in half as many weddings.

Over a period of eighty-two years the marriage rate in America has averaged almost exactly ten per one thousand population—that is, ten marriages a year per one thousand population. The marriage rate has been

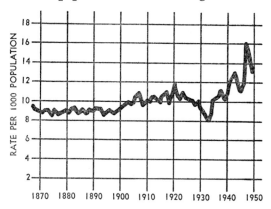

Fig. 1. Marriage Rates: United States, 1867-1948

The average marriage rate for the eighty-two year period has been 9.96 per 1,000 population. These estimates are based on special reports issued by the National Office of Vital Statistics.

above the average each year since 1934, reaching the peak of 16.4 per one thousand population in 1946. The marriage rate in 1867, at the beginning of the eighty-two year period, was 9.6. It did not go above ten until 1903 when it reached 10.1. The lowest rate of any year since 1867 was in the depression in 1932 when the rate was 7.9.

In the twenty year period from 1928 to 1947 the average marriage rate was 11.0, whereas in the twenty year period from 1867 to 1886 the average marriage rate was 8.97. This represents an increase of 2.03 as between the two twenty year periods.[1]

Nearly everybody gets married. If you live to be forty-five, the chances are nine to one that you will have a wedding day, for ninety per cent of all adults marry.

It is simply true that life is lived in society. We have acquaintances, associates, friends. The norm is for each mature person to have a boon companion for life and that one should live out his life not alone but in society —that is, with one person with whom he shares his life.

1. Handicaps Don't Hinder

People get married in spite of what would appear to be the grossest sort of personal handicaps. Even those with unusual physical deformity have married. So have the diseased, the ugly, and many with mean dispositions.

It is an experience affected little if any by circumstances of stature, complexion, health, wealth, intelligence, nationality, climate, education, or any other factor. The rich and the poor, the slim and the fat, the bald and the shaggy, the handsome and the ugly, the smart and the dumb, the young and the old—all are found at the altar.

It has always been true in all ages and among all peoples. No doubt it will continue to be so until we come

---

[1]These and other statistics on marriage are from reports of the National Office of Vital Statistics, Federal Security Agency, Washington, D. C.

to that unique land concerning which Jesus said, "In the resurrection they neither marry, nor are given in marriage."

2. *Quick Now: Do You Want to Get Married?*

Suppose you live in Oklahoma. It is pointed out to you that the marriage rate in your state is 9. Your informant also tells you that the rate in South Carolina is 23.6.

What would you say?

Would you exclaim, "I'm going to South Carolina!" Or would you exult, "I'm glad I live in Oklahoma!" Which would be the normal reaction?

Again suppose that you are a young lady living in Atlanta, Georgia. You learn that your prospects for marriage are lessened because there are only eighty-five men for every one hundred women in your city. But in Wyoming, you are told, there are one hundred and twenty-two men for every one hundred women. Will you begin packing your bag for a western journey?

Once more suppose that you are a young man on a farm in Missouri. Some friend reveals to you that only 85 per cent of the men in rural communities ever marry, whereas 92 per cent of the men who live in cities marry.

Will you begin at once to read the help wanted ads in the big city dailies?

Nearly everybody marries, and they do so willingly. People want to get married. Those who do, do so voluntarily as a mutually desired venture.

3. *More Facts in This Interesting Case*

In 1949, 84,323,000 citizens of the United States had been married. This was 57.2 per cent of the estimated population. It was 77.2 per cent of the population fourteen years old and over. The number of women exceeded the number of men by 1½ million (54,448,000 men, 56,001,000 women).

Women are more successful in getting married than are men, the 1949 report showing that 86.6 per cent of all women eighteen years old and above had been married compared with 80.2 per cent of men for the same ages. Now it is true that every time a woman marries some man stands by her side, but it still can be true that in the total population more women may experience marriage than men. This can be possible because of the factors of death and divorce. Thus we note that 44,827,-000 women over eighteen years old had ever been mar-

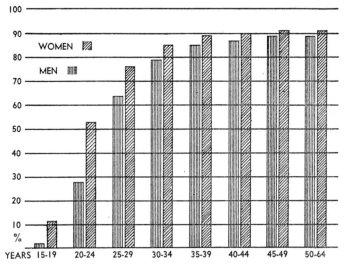

FIG. 2. PERCENTAGE WHO MARRY

Percentage of men and women who had ever married, by age periods, 1940. From Metropolitan Life Insurance Company, *Statistical Bulletin* (Feb. 1947).

ried in 1949 compared with 39,496,000 men, a difference of 5-1/3 million, or more than three times the excess of the total number of women over the total number of men.   It is also noted that 6,582,000 women were widowed compared with 2,181,000 men and that 1,233,-000 women were divorced compared with 842,000 men, a combined difference of 4,792,000 more women widowed and divorced than men.

Women marry younger than do men.   There are more women married in any age bracket from fourteen to thirty-nine, but above forty there are more men married.

The marriage career of women is more often terminated by the death of the companion than it is for men. This is true because of the shorter age span of a man's life.   Men on the average live some five years less than do women.   Since women also marry younger than do men, there is an average residue of some seven years in the life of the average woman which she may expect to live in widowhood. This situation is clearly revealed by the statistics which show that there are more women who are widowed of all ages than there are men.   This is true both numerically and by percentage.   For instance, the total number of women fourteen years old and over in 1949 who had been widowed, 6,582,000, was 4.4 per cent of the total population; males fourteen years old and over who were widowed, 2,181,000, totaled only 1.4 per cent of the population.

At fifty-five years and over 39.3 per cent of the women were widowed, whereas only 14.9 per cent of the men had lost their wives.

4. Marriage and Geography

People get married in all sections regardless of terrain or climate.   There are some sharp differences in the marriage rate between adjacent states, usually because of differences in marriage laws. For instance, Tennessee, which required a three day wait before issuance of license, has consistently had a low marriage rate, ranking at the bottom in a recent year with only 5.6 marriages per one thousand population. Neighboring Kentucky, with no period of waiting, had a marriage nearly five times as great, 25.8 per one thousand. It is necessary, therefore, to study larger areas than states for an understanding of any effect of geography upon marriage.

The mountain states had a marriage rate in 1947 of 32.4 per thousand, more than twice that of the entire nation. Even when allowance is made for the unusual number of remarriages in Nevada (which explains the phenomenal total of 411.1 marriages per one thousand) it is still true that marriages in the great mountain section of the west surpass the rest of the nation. Standing second in the sectional ratings with 17.5 per one thousand is the East South Central region, comprising the states of Kentucky, Tennessee, Alabama, and Mississippi. Other regions above the national average are the South Atlantic (16.0) and the West South Central (16.0).

Regions that are below the national average are the West North Central (12.9), East North Central (12.5), New England (12.0), Middle Atlantic (11.3), and, at the bottom, the Pacific states (10.8).

It is apparent, therefore, that the marriage rate is high in open agricultural and ranching regions. The rate is low in industrial sections. The five highest states are Nevada, 411.1; Arizona, 39.0; Maryland, 27.2; New Mexico 26.9; Kentucky, 25.8. The five lowest states are Tennessee, 5.6; Oregon, 8.4; North Carolina, 9.1; Oklahoma, 9.2; California, 9.6.

5. *United States Leads in Marriage*

The prospects for marriage are greater in the United States than in most of the countries of the Western world. This fact is revealed by studies made by the Metropolitan Life Insurance Company.[2]

Women in the United States, the studies show, have better chances of marriage at any age than do the women of any of the other fifteen nations, according to the latest census in each country. At age forty-five 91 per cent of our women are married, with Canada and France not far behind. Lowest here and for every other age is the Irish Free State with only 74 per cent. American women also marry earlier, 12 per cent of those fifteen to nineteen years of age being married, which was twice as high as in France and Canada, the two countries most closely approaching the American experience. In Italy, Belgium, Portugal, and Australia the figure was 4 per cent. The poorest prospects for early marriage in the sixteen countries studied existed in pre-war Germany, Irish Free State, and Norway where only 1 per cent of girls fifteen to nineteen were married. By age twenty-four more than half of the women in the United States are married—nearly twice the number in England and Wales and considerably over four times the 12 per cent total in Ireland.

Men also marry younger in the United States, 2 per cent being married by age nineteen whereas in only three of the nations studied—Denmark, Belgium, and France—does the total reach as high as 1 per cent. By age twenty-four 28 per cent of American men are married, the next high nation being France with 21 per cent and Ireland being low with only 3 per cent. Of the six-

---

[2]From the *Statistical Bulletin,* Metropolitan Life Insurance Company, February, 1947.

teen nations studied, the Irish Free State ranks at the bottom in percentage of marriages for every age, for both men and women. The United States ranks at the head of the list for every age of women and equals or exceeds all other nations in all ages for men through thirty-four.

6. *Your Chances of Marriage*

At birth in the United States the chances of eventual marriage for a girl are slightly more than eight out of

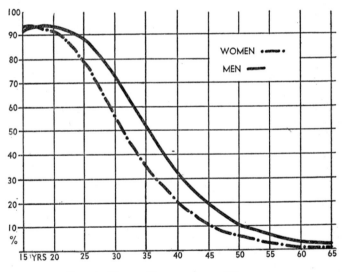

FIG. 3. YOUR CHANCES OF MARRIAGE

The percentage who ever marry, based on population reports of the Bureau of the Census, for the period 1920-1939. The percentage represents the total chance of marriage for persons who have attained the specified age.

ten.[3] For a boy the chances are somewhat less than eight out of ten. At age five the prospects for both have increased slightly. At age ten, ninety girls out of one hundred will eventually marry and about eighty-three boys out of one hundred. The peak in chances of eventual marriage is reached between ten and fifteen and declines slightly for boys and more definitely for girls for the next five years.

After twenty-two, chances of marriage for both men and women decline sharply. At thirty, the chances for men are about seventy-two out of one hundred and for women about fifty-five out of one hundred. At forty about thirty men out of one hundred eventually marry and twenty women.

In the early years the chances of eventual marriage for girls are greater than for boys, but after twenty the chances for men exceed the chances of women. This is because women marry earlier than do men and in most marriages the husband is older than the wife.

III. SOCIETY DEMANDS IT

Marriage is a social inevitable. It is the one basic socially unifying factor in man's life on earth. No institution in human society is more fundamental—not government, for law and order are needed only because of a society which already exists by reason of marriage; not the school, for education is a function of the home even before social organization brought the first school into existence; not even the church, even though its spiritual mission is admittedly of the greatest importance; but marriage, which commits a man and a woman to live together as long as

---

[3]These calculations are based on population reports of the Bureau of the Census, November 21, 1945, for the period 1920-1939.

life lasts, is the basic social institution. For society, in truth, is togetherness, association, the interplay of human personality; in fact, it is the good art of living one with another in a shared life. Marriage is the initiation of such relation and the home which results therefrom is the first unit in all of society.

1. *Fundamental in Social Organization*

Any general trend toward failure to marry would amount to a general avoidance of mature social responsibility. Its end result would be a denial of social existence, even as deliberate avoidance of parenthood after marriage is appropriately called "race suicide." A social policy which leaves out marriage is one which would terminate social organization just as certainly as an adult policy which prevents the birth of children kills the race. It is hardly strong enough, therefore, to say that society demands marriage. Actually, society exists because of marriage. Marriage is fundamental to all social organization. It has been so in all ages of history, among all classes of men, and in all races of humankind.

The expectation of society (of parents) is that children shall become fullgrown and take their mature places in society. Entrance into maturity and full assumption of the responsibilities of adulthood are signified in the popular mind by marriage. This expectation is to be fulfilled in spite of any extenuating circumstances, whether social or personal. Indeed marriage records show that these so-called extenuating circumstances operate nearly always only as delaying factors and not with permanent effect on marriage either generally or to individuals. For instance, sickness or vocational training may delay marriage, but seldom would either circumstance or any similar situation prevent ultimate marriage. Depression or war may cause a general delay or accentuation of marriage as has been true in this country more than once in this century, but again the effect is temporary. However, there may be a long range effect on marriage from continuing economic conditions, as is evidenced today in the two extreme cases of the United States and the Irish Free State. The low marriage rate in Ireland (70 per cent for men and 76 per cent for women) is very likely the result of the continuing pressure of hard times and a prevailing social policy which results in many adults remaining unmarried. In contrast, the high marriage rate in the United States (90 per cent of all adults) is at least in part the result of favorable economic conditions. But in each nation marriage is still the norm with from three-fourths to nine-tenths of all adults marrying.

2. *Social Disturbance and Marriage*

Social disturbance emphasizes the need of the family and the institution of marriage by which the family is established. In fact, the more pronounced the social upheaval, the more is marriage accented. When pestilence sweeps the land, when catastrophe strikes a city, when war spreads destruction abroad, when depression stalks as a specter, then society needs the unifying, conserving, enheartening influence of the family. This fact is dramatized graphically in time of war, for even as men hurry away to the battlefields they seek the anchorage of the home through sometimes hasty and ill-advised marriages, and when they return from battle again they see in marriage and home the way to security from the ravages of war. Revolution, whether industrial, agrarian, cultural, or military, accents the function and need of marriage. Society holds together in the family, even against any and all disturbing social upheavals.

There is an apparent conflict here. Society demands marriage, and yet social conditions oftentimes are not favorable to marriage. Economic conditions especially may discourage marriage and parenthood—and this in spite of the axiomatic fact that social organization demands marriage. The point to remember is that there is a difference between social conditions and social necessity. That is, circumstances may often be in apparent conflict with the drive toward absolute necessity. In any realm of human behavior there are always checks and balances, and one reaches his goal in any endeavor by overcoming counter forces.

Now society demands marriage as a general policy. But social conditions at the moment may oppose marriage generally or for the individual personally. Actually this is not as paradoxical as it would at first seem nor is the seeming conflict insuperable. To say that public education demands teachers, for instance, is not to assert that everyone must teach nor that those who enter the classroom must begin at any specified age. There are other necessities also operating with reference to qualification. Even so there are limiting factors in marriage. Society as a way of life demands marriage, but the individual knows other demands also which limit and delay his entry into marriage and through which he must fight his way through to the goal.

If the limiting factors become too great, society should adopt a policy aimed at overcoming them. In some situations, both as a community action and to relieve individual cases, steps may be needed which will encourage both marriage and parenthood. In general, since the average marriage age has decreased more than two years since 1890, it would seem that such steps are not needed in the United States, except perhaps in some communities and with reference to certain cases, such as that of students who face many years of preparation for the professions.

Marriage is a social inevitable, as necessary to society as eating or sleeping is to the individual. Society lays down no exaction with reference to position, personality, or heredity. Those who grow to maturity are expected to mark their entry into full adulthood through marriage. This is the logical, the necessary, the inevitable expectation of society.

IV. Human Personality Requires It

Volumes of truth are contained in the Scripture text, "It is not good that the man should be alone" (Gen. 2:18). God knew that he had created a gregarious creature who would prosper by companionship and suffer without it.

In this text is a volume on physiology. Human health is improved by marriage. Studies show that married men and women live longer and enjoy better health than do the unmarried.

Here is a volume on psychology. Loneliness is not good for mental health. The normal person soon wearies of a hermit's life. A smaller percentage of the married are committed to institutions for the insane and for nervous disorders than of the unmarried. It is not good for man to be alone for psychic reasons.

This one Scripture sentence speaks volumes on economics. Married persons make a better record of economic success than do the unmarried. Marriage is a help and almost never a hindrance to men in any trade, business, or profession. The married person is more stable, he belongs more to the community, and in general, he gives better service to his employer, thus justifying the larger financial returns claimed by the married.

Living alone is not successful for the human spirit. Human personality was created for the companionship

of marriage.   One of the inalienable rights not mentioned
in the Constitution is the human prerogative of marriage.
No man lives to himself alone.   Viewed from the standpoint of personal needs, marriage is the normal aim and
desire of all.

V. God Designed It

God designed this human institution as the normal
experience of men and women.   He created woman as
an helpmeet to man and man as a companion and husband to his wife.   The two complement each other. They
were made for each other.   No person in all the world
is so interesting, so attractive, so amiable, so lovable as
the woman of a man's choice.   Nor is there anyone to a
woman so strong, so noble, so helpful, so true as the man
with whom she has joined her life until death shall part
them.

This is according to God's good purpose for humankind.   He created the affinity between man and woman.
He sparked the interest between the first two, abetted
the association which developed into courtship and finally issued in an impelling lifetime bond of affection, and
crowned the first wedding by himself performing the
ceremony.

It is no wonder, therefore, that most people do marry,
that those who are wise enter into such a union perma-
nently, that the strength of their union grows with the
passing years.   It is no wonder that this relation brings
the supreme happiness known in human relations.   It is
no wonder that Christian marriage based upon Christian
principles and resulting in the establishment of a Christian home brings about a very heaven on earth.

SOME THINGS TO THINK ABOUT

1. Which is more important, choosing a vocation or a mate? Which usually receives more attention?
2. Should one pray about marriage choice?
3. Suggest reasons for the increase in the marriage rate in this country.
4. Discuss the personal and social significance of the fact that more women are widowed than men.
5. In general, should marriage be encouraged or discouraged in the United States?
6. Is Christian marriage the finest fellowship in human relations?

Chapter II

What Marriage Means

Whoso findeth a wife findeth a good thing, and obtaineth favour of the Lord.—PROVERBS 18:22.

Suppose you are establishing a business partnership. Before entering into the arrangement you will have a full understanding about the details of the partnership—the capital each will invest, the responsibilities each will assume, the division of earnings, conditions governing termination of the partnership. It would be utter folly to set up a business partnership without working out these details in advance. A full understanding is required in a business relationship.

A clear view on marriage is likewise a necessity. If one needs full knowledge of the conditions involved in a business venture, it is even more urgent that he should have a full understanding of the conditions involved in a lifelong companionship. A business entered into haphazardly does not give much promise of success, nor does a marriage hold out much hope of fulfilling the joys anticipated and divinely intended unless the two have a full understanding of the relation into which they are entering. The meaning of marriage is an appropriate study for all Christian young people.

I. A CHRISTIAN INTERPRETATION

Three principal passages summarize the New Testament teachings on marriage. These are Matthew 19:3-12, 1 Corinthians 7, and Ephesians 5:22-33. There are related passages—the teachings in Matthew 19 being included at least in part in Matthew 5:27-31, Mark 10:2-12, and Luke 16:18; 1 Corinthians 7 being at least in part an enlargement of similar teachings in 1 Corinthians 5 and 6; and the message of Ephesians 5 being summarized in Colossians 3:18-19—but these three passages in Matthew 19, 1 Corinthians 7, and Ephesians 5 set forth the New Testament teachings on marriage.

Even a hasty look at these passages reveals at once that two of them were provoked by questioners. In Matthew the ugly spirited Pharisees prodded Jesus with the divorce question in the hope of trapping him. Their interest was not in the institution of marriage but only in destroying this prophet who taught contrary to their traditions. But even in that vile atmosphere Jesus lifts marriage to the high plane divinely intended by the One who performed the first wedding ceremony. Questions raised by the Corinthians and discussed by Paul in his seventh chapter evidently grew out of simple ignorance and an honest desire to know the answer. This type of inquiry is prerequisite to a discovery of the truth. When one raises questions out of an open mind and with an honest desire to know the answers, he is ready to be taught. Those who are in a position to teach are eager to respond and will do so helpfully. We may well cultivate this spirit of straightforward inquiry into the meaning of marriage.

1. *Jesus on Stability in Marriage*

As we have already noted, the question of the Pharisees was another of their repeated efforts to trap Jesus. There were two popular views in interpretation of their query, "Is it lawful for a man to put away his wife for every cause?" (Matt. 19:3). One school of thought interpreted "every cause" literally—it might be the way a woman dressed her hair, or set the table, or did or did not

trim her fingernails—any cause which the man might state
was regarded as sufficient grounds. The other school of
thought contended for a more rigid application; a man
should not give his wife a writing of divorcement for any
little inconsequential matter but only because of moral
uncleanness even as Moses in the law had specified.

Now the gleeful Pharisees were confident that they had
forced on Jesus a dilemma neither horn of which he could
afford to take. The clash between these two schools of
thought was so sharp that if he accepted either view he
would thereby antagonize the other group. Jesus not
only with consummate skill evaded both horns of the
dilemma but gave the superlative Christian message on
stability in marriage. That message gives the sanctity
to the home characteristic of Christian society.

In essence Jesus said that entry into marriage with
any thought that it is to be temporary—that a man shall
put away his wife for any "cause"—does injury to the institution of marriage. Actually such a relation is to be
terminated only by one or the other of two factors:
death—which he does not specifically mention—and a
violation of the singlehearted abandonment each to the
other which made them one.

(1) *His fourfold argument.*—Permanence in marriage
Jesus supports with a fourfold argument. First, the "duo-
humanity" of male and female requires it. The one was
made for the other. The two complement each other.
The highest good of each is fulfilled in association with
the other—psychologically, emotionally, physically, spiritually, socially. Second, the utter abandonment which
marks entry into marriage argues for its perpetuation.
With joy and eager anticipation a son will depart from
his natural family to form a new relation based on choice.
Such a spirit of abandonment should rule out any consideration of termination of the new union. Third, their

union has become an accomplished fact, for "they are no more twain, but one flesh." Fourth, this union is sealed by divinity—"what therefore God has joined together"—and no man, be he king or priest, dares set it aside except at the risk of doing a great evil.

(2) *His explanation of Moses' sufferance.*—In rebuttal, the Pharisees cite their key text. Those who argue can always cite chapter and verse, and they can use it to serve their own selfish ends. Moses had provided for a "writing of divorcement" (Deut. 24:1), but it is necessary to understand the conditions under which the law was given, to which conditions Jesus alludes when he speaks of "the hardness of your hearts."

The laws of Moses were given to a people who had been slaves. As has always marked the society of slaves, the institution of marriage was corrupted; morals were at a low ebb. The Israelites, though they were God's chosen people, were a rather sorry lot socially. Now Moses was a spiritual leader who by revelation gave them a moral code which was idealistic: thou shalt not steal, thou shalt not kill, thou shalt not bear false witness, thou shalt not commit adultery. Moses was also a political and civic ruler who had to write laws to apply in the day-by-day life of a people who had come out of slavery. The Israelites could and did escape from bondage to the Egyptians overnight, but they could not or did not step at once into the full-orbed standard of ethical living which marks a spiritually cultured society. They continued to divorce in the scandalous manner characteristic of slaves. Moses found it necessary for the protection of women who were thus abandoned and as a forward step in moral progress to set up regulations governing this ugly reality. It was indeed for the hardness of their hearts that Moses "suffered" these primitive former slaves to put away their wives, "but," says Jesus, "from the beginning it was not so."

(3) *His firm plea for permanence.*—Jesus concludes his annunciation of the permanence of marriage by asserting that it is a bond so strong that in its very nature no factor can bring about severance except only actual infidelity on the part of one of the parties to the union.

Jesus definitely and vigorously opposed the loose attitudes toward marriage prevalent in his day. He taught that marriage is indissoluble from its very nature and from its divine appointment as he set marriage on its true foundation and spoke for the sanctity of the home. Not only had the laxity which prevailed in pagan Rome spread to Palestine—some scribes even holding that divorce was a special dispensation granted to Jews only—but the monarch himself was a flagrant offender. It was a decision on this dangerous question of divorce which had brought death to the forerunner, for it was in consequence of John the Baptist's fearless denunciation of Herod, "it is not lawful for you to have her," that his head was finally brought forth on a charger to please the adulteress whom he had offended.

2. *Paul's Reply to Corinthians*

Passing now to the Corinthian passage we find two questions which also reflect the spirit of the times. The first was, Should one marry at all? And the second, If married, should one remain married? Each was addressed to Paul by the Christians at Corinth in utter sincerity and ignorance and reflects the conditions of the day. Marriage in the wicked city of Corinth had sunk to low levels. Divorce was widespread. Immorality was rampant. Home life was at a low ebb—so much so that pure-minded Christians might properly shun marriage itself. The first question of the Corinthian Christians grew out of this setting. But the point of the question turned on the presumed superior virtues of the single state over marriage for a Christian in such a community.

The second question was somewhat related in context. Each convert was a first generation Christian who came to Christ out of this environment. Each, of course, responded to the gospel individually, and frequently his wife or husband did not join him in genuine repentance and faith. Thus many households were divided on the matter of religion—and the division was pronounced, the lines being drawn sharply between the high ethical standards of Christianity and the low morals of the day. In such a situation should a Christian remain married to his unbelieving wife or husband?

In reply to the first question Paul expands the teachings of Jesus in Matthew 19:10-12. There, in response to a similar question, Jesus had pointed out that disability of one form or another may prevent some from marrying while others choose to remain single in the interest of greater kingdom usefulness. Neither marriage nor failure to marry, Jesus points out, is a virtue in itself, but only that marital decision has special value which is based upon the greatest possible kingdom service.

In like manner Paul says that every man must determine for himself what is best. He does indicate a personal bias that all might be as he was (that is, single) for the sake of the kingdom, but he entertained no illusions that all or even a majority would elect such a course. Neither does he imply that supreme happiness will come to everyone automatically through marriage. He does not teach that everyone *must* marry. Rather each one should consider his own bent, and, as a Christian, reach a decision to marry or not to marry according to the dictates of his own spirit and the leading of the Lord.

To the second question Paul's reply is pointed. He pleads that the marriage state be kept intact. The Christian is not to break it because his companion is an unbeliever. Indeed the believer will bring a testimony which may win his companion to faith in Christ.

3. *Marital Devotion of Christians*

In the Ephesian epistle Paul sets forth the basis of Christian marriage. It is a relation comparable in both directions to the relation between Christ and his bride, the church. The devotion of the wife to her husband is "as unto the Lord." With full confidence in his integrity, in his character, in his moral capacity, she reposes her welfare in her husband's keeping. This submission and utter confidence is not as unto one who lords it over her like a tyrant, but even as a believer reposes implicit confidence in his Lord. Now it is not specifically stated here but plainly implied that she has found one who is trustworthy, even as the believer has been convinced of the trustworthiness of the Lord Jesus Christ. Thus the testing point of the teaching turns both ways: the wife is full of faith in her husband and remains true in her fidelity, but the husband is faithful, meriting the trust by his own integrity and fidelity.

In like manner the love of the husband for his wife is compared to the love of Christ for his church. Even as Christ gave himself for weak and helpless sinners, so Christian husbands are to love and cherish their wives.

Such a mutuality of high devotion is the basis for Christian marriage, for Paul concludes that "for this cause shall a man leave his father and mother, and shall be joined unto his wife." The young man who is worthy of the maid he woos must bring her a pledge of such true devotion. The young woman is not ready to stand at the marriage altar unless and until she can return such deep and lasting affection in kind. Only the marriage based on such a singlehearted fidelity gives promise of resulting in all that God intended for this holy institution. Of course, such an affection ripens through the experiences of the years, but it should be present in definite promise in those days of courtship which lead to a pledge of marriage.

Paul assumes here that the parties are Christians, that each is such in character as to make possible the "love" on one side and the "reverence" on the other. Right here is the essential element in this Christian law of marriage, namely, that each party to the relation shall recognize the duty of cultivating a character worthy of the "love" and the "reverence" which are enjoined.

4. Summary of Paul's Teachings

These passages from Paul may be summarized under the four basic marital questions.

(1) *Should one marry?*—It is a question which should not be settled arbitrarily but relatively. The answer depends upon oneself, upon finding another who is prepared to enter into marriage with him, on what the two can put into marriage together, and on what the entire relation will mean to their work for the Lord. It is to be decided on the basis of personal aptitudes, personality, and purpose in life, even as also are all other questions. What one should do in any given situation is never to be answered generally but specifically, personally. Some do not *want* to get married; they need not feel that they must. If one does not want to marry a certain person, it would be supremely tragic for him to do so. Most people want to get married; most people finally do get married; but no one should feel that he is forced into marriage apart from a personal, voluntary

decision reached ultimately in consideration with the person of his choice.

(2) *Whom should one marry?*—Again the answer is relative and very personal. In general Christians will marry "in the Lord" and will avoid being "unequally yoked together." Religion shared in the home brings great blessings. Spiritual compatibility is the basis for great family happiness. Thus as the Christian approaches marriage he will do well to do so among those who share his religious views.

(3) *On what basis should one marry?*—Only a true devotion, addressed with singlehearted purpose to one individual and issuing in a pledge of lifetime devotion is the right basis for entry into marriage.

(4) *If married to an unbeliever or otherwise unhappily joined together, then what?*—The message is clear. Stay together. Society must have the solid foundation of permanence in marriage. Even though one may be married to an unbeliever he is to remain faithful, using every opportunity of home ties to bring his unsaved companion to the Saviour. Marriage is a relation so fundamental in the social structure that it is to be severed only by moral unfaithfulness or death itself.

5. *Christian Standards for Marriage*

On the basis of these and similar or related passages four great ethical principles stand out. These may be thought of as setting forth the Christian standards for marriage.

(1) *Monogamy.*—"A man . . . shall be joined unto his wife"—each noun is singular. The very nature of marriage, the pure moral standard which is required as its predicate, the supreme devotion which marks its course, the one ground of unfaithfulness which alone terminates

the bond, argue for monogamy. One man shall be married to one wife—not one man to three women, nor one woman to five men (even though it may be in the Hollywood pattern). Human experience confirms the scriptural standard of one husband being joined to one wife.

(2) *Permanence.*—Even from the beginning, said Jesus, "it was not so." Divorce is an innovation marking man's downward trend of depravity. Stability in marriage is a social necessity, and the permanence of the bond is the clear teaching Christ laid down for his followers.

(3) *Perfect chastity.*—There can be no double standard in Christian society. Each party to marriage should bring to the altar a perfect record of moral behavior, no blemish marking the life of either, and each being faithful to the other in a lifetime devotion. Any deviation is a deadly sin, breaking the bond itself. This is the rigid, undeviating Christian standard of morality.

(4) *Based on love.*—In marriage the Christian couple ardently desire each other. Their union does not hold together either by reason of social pressure or legal requirement. They have entered into the union because of a lasting mature devotion which they cultivate and which ripens with the passing of the happy years. Here is the surpassing element in Christian marriage—the sort of devotion which can be compared even to the love of Christ for the church.

II. WHAT MARRIAGE MEANS TO YOU

The foregoing study of the New Testament teaching on marriage is objective in approach. We come now to a more subjective viewpoint. What will actual marriage mean to you as an experience?

1. *A New Type of Companionship*

An evangelist was preaching on heaven. "It will be a new relation," he said. "We have nothing in our present experience to make us know what heaven will be like. It will be different from anything heretofore experienced. For instance, before my wife and I married we knew that we loved each other, and we very much wanted to be married, but not until we actually were married could we ever know the meaning of this new relation entered at marriage. Again, we wanted children, we prayed for children, but we could not know the meaning of the new relation of parents until after the first little one came to bless our home."

Marriage brings a new type of companionship, one the full import of which can never be comprehended short of actual experience. Heretofore your entire life has been in the natural family—that is, the family to which you were born. You are a child to you parents, an older brother or younger sister to other members of the family. Your family has been a kinship group, parents and children bound together by blood ties.

At marriage you will enter a family different both in type and in relation to anything you have heretofore experienced. It may be called an artificial family—not one bound together by blood ties, but one volitionally established. Not now as a child or yet as a brother or a sister—not as an inferior or as a superior—but as two equals you will face life together. The equality of relationship is novel. Never before have you known a family relationship with another as equals.

Also for the first time in your life you will assume the initiative in family administration. Now it is *your* family. Now the initiative in all family decisions rests upon you and your companion. Before you may have voiced an opinion and as a child your judgment may have been considered, but now the primary burden of initiative and performance in family affairs rests alike upon you and your companion in a shared responsibility.

This new type of companionship between equals is voluntarily assumed. Most people want to get married and most people do get married, but in the normal setting today each one enters it of his own accord. The relation is also one of interdependence. The wife depends upon the husband; the husband depends upon the wife; but each must stand for himself in character and behavior as becomes the mature Christian person that he should be. Each is independent both in the home and out of it as a full-grown individual, but each also is surely dependent on the other day by day.

Unique also is the affectional quality of this new relation. One selects a friend because of admired qualities. One knows acquaintances simply by reason of the casual crosscurrents of life. One enters into a business partnership on the basis of economic considerations. One selects a roommate because of congeniality. All of these factors or qualities are involved in marriage—these, plus something more. It is something for which there is no adequate word in any language. Marriage is entered into because of mutual respect, admiration, confidence, love— because of a compelling urgency for each other which makes two determined to share their lives together.

That is what marriage is—a sharing of life. There is no other relation like it. Two people do not marry in order to accomplish goals, although each will give himself with utter abandonment to the accomplishment of common goals, whether economic, cultural, spiritual, physical, or social. The goals, vocational or otherwise, are incidental to the marriage. They marry to live together, whether the husband be a farmer, rancher, merchant, lawyer, or minister. Shared living issuing from an ardent desire for each other epitomizes this new type of companionship.

2. *Mark of Maturity*

Marriage ordinarily is an experience at the threshold of maturity. More than any other it is the one step signifying full development to manhood's estate and an assumption of the responsibilities of maturity. Of course, it does not imply the full maturity of later years but it is in a real sense a commencement of the well-rounded experiences of adulthood.

Nor should marriage be thought of necessarily as exclusive in the sense that it alone marks maturity. Those who do not marry do not thereby prove themselves to be immature; they have simply not entered into the experience which more than any other is commonly recognized as marking life's larger and mature responsibilities. The normal social state of a man is as husband and father. The usual and fundamental place of woman in society is as wife and mother. Marriage recognizes this norm and thrusts man and woman into the adult years of normal mature relationship.

3. *Acceptance of Basic Fact of Life*

The science textbooks carry interesting illustrations of the life cell. First the single cell is a distinct unity. Then there is a discernible impulse toward division which grows until a separation occurs forming two cells. Again for each new cell the process is repeated, and so on endlessly. This process in reverse illustrates the ongoing of human life, which issues not from a single individual but from a psychic, emotional, physical, and spiritual union so real as to provoke the scriptural description, "the twain shall become one flesh."

The individual finds himself in a continuing stream of life. His marriage is a definite part of it and acceptance of the very reality of existence. Marriage is a wholesome, healthy, optimistic view of life. "I am alive!" exclaims the person marrying. "I am a part of a continuing stream of life. I rejoice in it. I will not be a party to the termination of this stream, but gladly I take my place in its continuance."

Any other view is one of intolerable pessimism. Any other policy brings death to society. Any other deliberate and general course would put an end to the human family on earth.

It is inspiring that the human race characteristically faces life optimistically in a ready acceptance of the reality of existence and of mature responsibility in the ongoing of life.

4. *Change of Residence*

Marriage brings a somewhat radical change of residence. You will move from the home of your parents into a home of your own. Very likely it will be from the conveniences and comforts marking your parents' accumulation during their married lifetime into the simple surroundings which a young couple ordinarily can afford. This may be a drastic change, for the parents' home represents savings of a lifetime and the modest furnishings of the new quarters will reflect the limited resources of the newlyweds. No longer will you know the comforts and some luxuries which your parents can afford. Living quarters will be simpler and less expensive. Indeed the whole standard of living is likely to be reduced in a manner which may prove irksome. To say the least, there will be a sharp change in the physical setting of your living quarters.

5. *Change of Home Associations*

Marriage means separation from the family of your childhood. Daily, almost hourly, association with mother is no longer possible. The reassuring presence of father in the early morning and late evening is no longer known. Family living with brothers and sisters is a thing of the past. Now you will enter into a family of your own with the companion of your choice, thus marking new associations different from the ones of old and to be retained throughout the remainder of life.

6. *Economic Reorganization*

There will be little, if any, change in employment at marriage—except for the wife—but there will be a drastic reorganization of economic affairs. Before you have used all of your economic resources on self. You have put your entire salary in your own pocket and spent it at will. This can no longer be possible in partnership living. All that one earns is as much the other's as it is his own. Indeed it belongs actually to neither, but to both. Use of it will be governed by the basic rules of shared living. In this partnership living every question concerning finances will be faced together and the decision will not be an individual one but will be made as a pair together who order their lives as one.

III. What Marriage Means to Your Family

Scarcely any event in family living is as significant to this primary kinship group as is the marriage of one of its members. It is at once a time of joy and of departure, a time of laughter and of weeping, a time of exultation and of bewilderment. Happy that family that can take a wedding in stride.

Three words summarize and suggest some of the things that your marriage will mean to your family. First, *separation:* you are leaving; no longer will you be an active participant in family life; your place in the family as of yore is no more. Second, *independence:* now you are on your own for certain and for keeps; no longer are you subject to your parents; you will respect their judgment and seek their advice, but no longer will you look to them for the daily parental guidance which you have known all of your life. Third, *fulfilment:* you have come to the estate anticipated for you by your parents from your very earliest days; now they see you at the threshold of maturity assuming all of the prerogatives of adult life.

IV. What Marriage Means to Your Community

Society's stake in marriage is tremendous. The very structure of civilization rests upon it and the family established thereby. The many laws respecting marriage reflect the interest of the community in this institution. Marriage is an instance of social behavior which like all others must be governed by law, but in no other phase of social living is government so careful in the expression of the community's wishes.

Here it may be remarked that fools have rushed in where angels fear to tread, for the many laws making for easy breakup of the home and society's easy conscience in the matter of divorce seem in defiance of Jesus' mandate, "What therefore God hath joined together, let not man put asunder." It is true of course, that legal compulsion can never save the home but rather only the Christian approach to marriage of Ephesians 5 which alone can make marriage permanent. Divorce records are symptomatic of a deeper malady and give no true reflection of society's great concern in your marriage.

Here are three words to suggest something of what your marriage means to your community. First, *realiza-*

tion: you are recognized as a full-grown adult in the affairs of your community; you belong to the scheme of things for your neighborhood. Second, *expectation:* you are expected to discharge the duties of a mature citizen, of a breadwinner, or a housewife in the community; together you now occupy the status of a family. Third, *perpetuation:* your very marriage gives the community new assurance of survival; it foretells the continued existence and well-being of your neighborhood, the state, the nation.

SOME THINGS TO THINK ABOUT

1. Should young people have a clear view of the meaning of marriage?
2. Is permanence in marriage the greatest social need?
3. Is instability in marriage symptomatic of general social decay?
4. Have you known husbands and wives who loved each other in the manner described in Ephesians 5?
5. Does society have a stake in your marriage?

Chapter III

When You Are of Age

> *His parents answered them and said . . . he is of age; ask him: he shall speak for himself.*—JOHN 9:20-21.

> *One of the main reasons for failure in marriage is that people who have not grown up try to make a child's game out of it.*—PAUL POPENOE.[1]

> *Just when we become wise enough to handle the problems that beset a marriage in our intricate civilization, it would be difficult to say.*—MEYER F. NIMKOFF.[2]

Marriage is for adults. It is the most mature relation of adult experience. If you have come of age in experience, in viewpoint, in economic outlook, in social relationships, in vocational purpose, in religious faith, you are ready for marriage. If you are not full grown in any of these respects, the foundation of your marriage cannot be as secure as you will want it to be.

Most marriages which fail do so because of some form of immaturity—usually because of some lack of emotional balance. Immature people—even though perhaps twenty, thirty, or even forty years of age—have tried to make it a child's game, and it is no wonder that they have failed.

---

[1]Paul Popenoe, *Modern Marriage* (New York: Macmillan, 1946), p. 9.

[2]Meyer F. Nimkoff, *Marriage and the Family* (New York: Houghton Mifflin, 1947), p. 459.

Your age in years does not necessarily determine your maturity. Some people mature earlier than others. Maturity refers to your general outlook on life, the poise and congeniality of your social contacts, the judgment you display in crises.

Do you remember, for instance, the first dollar you ever earned? What did you do with it? Do you recall it now as a thrilling experience?

When did you first spend a night away from home?

How old were you the first time you rode a train or bus alone?

What was your first job?

Who was your first boy or girl friend?

Can you remember every exciting moment of your first date?

At what age did you begin to drive a car?

Were you excited by your first long distance telephone call? Your first telegram? What about your first day at college?

Have you ever thought seriously that you might some-day marry a certain person?

These experiences have marked your growth toward maturity. They have helped to prepare you step by step for adulthood. Now it is not the number or the scope of such experiences which add up to the total of maturity, but it is the manner in which you meet them. You prove your maturity by the poise, the confidence, and the triumph with which you relate yourself to the normal situations of life.

If one behaves as a child—temperamentally, irrational-ly, unsocially—then he is thought of as a child no matter how many birthdays he may have had. If he has put away childish things and behaves as a man, he is called a man.

I. How Old Are You?

Physically? The human body is a marvel of God's creation. It has remarkable powers for self-maintenance, for growth, for propagation. Its activities are manifold and its functions are bewildering. So magnificent is it that in the Christian the body becomes a temple of the Holy Spirit.

In its physical cycle the body knows infancy, childhood, adolescence, adulthood, and sinility. A most fascinating period is adolescence when the human body matures in size and function.

Physical development pointing quickly toward adult stature should also be accompanied by mature viewpoints toward this physical mechanism. As you become mature physically, you should also become mature in the care of your own body and in proper respect for the bodies of others—care and respect as befit the earthly residence of God's Spirit.

Socially? Your age here, as in every other respect, is not determined by the calendar. It is demonstrated by the poise, or lack of it, with which you move among people. Can you meet both men and women easily and congenially? Here is another mark of maturity regardless of age.

Intellectually? Mental capacity is one of the great gifts of human personality. The power to assimilate facts, to reason, to reach a judgment, and to determine action is a surpassing human quality. Maturity in this area is not signified necessarily by graduation from any college or university. Rather it is shown by the capacity for rational thinking and for action based on a reasonable weighing of all issues involved. If you act on the basis of good judgment you give evidence of intellectual maturity.

Physically

Socially

Intellectually

Emotionally

Spiritually

Fig. 4. How Old Are You?

Physically you should be mature in the care of your own body and in respect for others. Socially, can you meet both men and women easily? Intellectual maturity is shown by rational thinking and action based on weighing of all issues. Those who lack emotional maturity rarely achieve a happy marriage. Spiritual maturity can be attained only by definite commitment to Christian living.

Spiritually? Have you learned to pray? Not to pray aloud necessarily, or just follow a routine of private praying, but have you learned the real habit of prayer? Do you read the Bible regularly? Do you turn to it for definite help on specific problems? Do you practice a faithful stewardship both of time and of income? **Are** you committed to definite Christian activity as a principle of life?

A sincere affirmative to these questions indicates a spiritual growth which will stand you in good stead for marriage. Prayer is the expression of faith, living proof of trust in God. It is a spiritual attitude fundamental to all human relations, especially to marriage. The habit of Bible reading shows a teachableness which indicates that one will grow in every relation of life. The Christian steward has learned one of the most practical doctrines, the doctrine of property; he has stability with reference to material things; he knows that a man's life "consisteth not in the abundance of the things which he possesses." A commitment to Christian service, whether as a full-time Christian worker or as a Christian layman, is the right register of Christian conscience to God's evident leadership. Every day the Christian will seek to apply the principles of Christ in his conduct and relations.

These qualities indicate growth toward God. How old are you spiritually? It is a good question to ask as one thinks of marriage.

Emotionally? How you express yourself with your feelings is an important proof of your maturity. If you have sudden fits of anger, throw tantrums, and otherwise are easily ruffled, you are still immature emotionally. The emotions cover the strong range of feelings such as fear, anger, distrust, grief, joy, surprise, yearning.

Emotional maturity is most significant in determining your readiness to marry. People who lack it rarely achieve a happy marriage.

II. AT WHAT AGE DO PEOPLE MARRY?

People marry at almost all ages from early adolescence to the grave. Data assembled by the Bureau of the

Census[3] shows that out of 1,000 girls who have reached
the age of fifteen, 10 will get married within their fifteenth
year; 1 boy out of 1,000 will be married in the fifteenth
year. In the twentieth year 67 boys out of 1,000 and 155

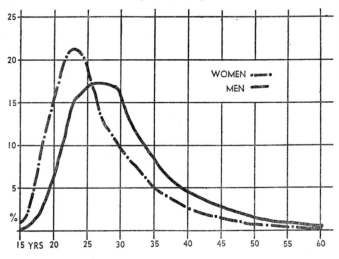

FIG. 5. MARRIAGES WITHIN YEAR

The percentage who marry within one year after
attaining specified age. This shows the chances
of marriage within one year after reaching any age
from 15 to 60. Based on data for period 1920-39,
Bureau of the Census, *Population—Special Reports*
(Nov. 21, 1945).

girls out of 1,000 will be married; in the twenty-fifth year
170 boys and 189 girls. The age of most frequent
marriages for men is twenty-seven and for women twenty-

[3]From *Population—Special Reports,* November 21, 1945. Based
on data for the period 1920-39.

three. However, marriages continue throughout life, at age sixty 5 men out of 1,000 and 2 women out of 1,000 experiencing marriage. Marriage for men usually occurs between twenty-five and twenty-seven years of age. For women marriage is an earlier experience, most women marrying before their twenty-fifth birthday. A nation-wide sample survey conducted by the Bureau of the Census[4] indicated that in 1947, 72 per cent of the male population and 84.6 per cent of the female population between twenty-five and thirty years of age had married. Of those between fourteen and twenty-five, 19 per cent of the men and 36 per cent of the women had married.

1. *They Marry Earlier Nowadays*

Contrary to popular belief, the average age of marriage has shown a steady decline in recent years, especially for men. In 1890, the median age at first marriage for all men who ever marry was 26.1[5]. In 1940 it was 24.3. For women there has been a very small decrease, from 22.0 in 1890 to 21.3 in 1930; in the next decade, or by 1940, the median age of first marriage for women had risen to 21.6. The trend toward earlier marriage is also shown in the proportion of young persons who are married. In 1890, 18.5 per cent of all persons between fifteen and twenty-four years of age were married; in 1940, the number was 23 per cent. In 1940, there were over 16,000 marriages in which the bride was under sixteen years of age.

The trend toward earlier marriage does not necessarily prove that young people are maturing earlier. Social experiences may hasten marriage. The likelier explanation is that favorable economic conditions have made early marriage practically possible.

---

[4]Current Population Reports, February 6, 1948.
[5]Nimkoff, *op. cit.,* p. 460.

"Finances," Paul Popenoe writes[6], "are an important part of the whole story, but the determination of bride and groom is what pulls the trigger."

In other words, people marry when they want to marry and when they think circumstances are favorable. In the United States in the past sixty years the trend has been toward earlier marriages because people generally have wanted to get married earlier and because conditions have made it possible for them to do so.

2. Social Status and Age of Marriage

Age of marriage is affected by social background and especially by education and vocation. Generally, rural people marry earlier than city dwellers, the uneducated marry earlier than the skilled, and the lower classes marry earlier than the upper classes.

One study[7] shows that 22 per cent of the women who drop out of school with less than five years of education are married before they reach twenty, while only 5 per cent of the women with a college education marry that early. By age forty-nine 96 per cent of the women with less than a fifth grade education were married, compared with 30 per cent of women with college education. College education limits a woman's chances of marriage. This is to be expected for at least two reasons. First, the vocational atmosphere of education encourages career aims; and, second, many women who go to college have ambitions other than homebuilding.

A long period of professional or vocational training has a delaying influence on marriage; for both men and women it limits the eventual possibility of marriage. Col-

---

[6]Popenoe, *op. cit.*, p. 9.

[7]Judson T. Landis and Mary G. Landis, *The Marriage Handbook* (New York: Prentice-Hall, 1948), p. 108.

lege marriages increased sharply for some years after the
war, due largely to the educational provisions in the G. I.
Bill of Rights and also to the fact that many young men
delayed both their education and their marriage because
of war. Marriage once was practically unknown on the
college campus; many colleges automatically expelled
students who married. There is now a new attitude
toward student marriage which perhaps will become
permanent. The popular view seems to be that if a
couple can work out their economic responsibilities, and
are sure they want to be married, they need not delay
until after graduation.

3. *Age Differences in Marriage*

At the normal age of marriage—that is, around twenty-
five or under twenty-seven for the man and around
twenty-two for the woman—there is an age difference of
about three years. In perhaps 80 per cent of the marriages the husband is older than the wife. The remaining 20 per cent is about equally divided, in 10 per cent
the wife being older and in 10 per cent the two being
the same age.

Women are at a disadvantage, however, beyond the
median age of marriage, for men as they grow older tend
to select wives who are more than three years younger.
At thirty-five, for instance, men do not ordinarily select
wives of thirty-two but of twenty-seven; at forty the
average man will not marry a woman of thirty-seven but
one of thirty-one years of age.

Actually any age difference either way need not be a
matter of consequence. The husband need not be older.
Indeed some studies indicate that the greatest happiness
is achieved when the wife is older. Others show that
there is great happiness when the husband is several
years older. The conclusion of those who have made

these studies is that it is doubtful that age difference is a factor of great importance in marital happiness.

III. What Is the Best Age for Marriage?

You are eager to know the best age at which you should marry. Nimkoff in *Marriage and the Family* raises the question but wants to know, "best for what?" There is need for clarification on Nimkoff's serious point.

There is a great deal of discussion about happiness in marriage as if the one aim in marriage is the attainment of personal happiness. Marriage for personal satisfaction only is a low goal, unworthy of a Christian who lives in the light of social responsibility and with the purpose of knowing and doing God's will. The successful Christian marriage does bring happiness to the husband and wife—perhaps the superlative joys in human relations— but no Christian would want to enter into marriage on the basis only of what would bring him the most pleasure.

1. *A Guiding Principle*

The best age for marriage, therefore, you will consider from the standpoint of what is best for the one you would marry, the best for your family, the best for your community, the best in the light of the total Christian service that you expect to render under God's leadership.

On the basis of this general guiding principle a study can be made of the principal scientific surveys in this field. These surveys show in general that the best age for women to marry seems to be between twenty-one and twenty-five. For men the best age seems to be between twenty-five and thirty. Under twenty-two for men and under twenty for women seems to be a dangerous risk. Youthful marriages are much more likely to end in divorce.

Age alone, of course, is not the sole factor in the higher number of failures among youthful marriages. Those who marry early usually are lacking in other elements of maturity, particularly emotional, which would increase the possibility of unhappiness in their marriages at any age. "Emotionally unstable, headstrong, self-willed young people, determined to have their own way at any cost," Paul Popenoe suggests in an article in *Parent's Magazine*, "Should College Students Marry?", July, 1938, "are not likely to marry successfully at any age, but if they do marry, are perhaps more likely to do so at twenty than at thirty." Often those who marry early rush into it because of some unhappy home situation or because of some other personality pressure.

2. *Marriage Under Pressure Is a Great Hazard*

Early marriages are often handicapped at the outset less by the youth of bride and groom than by the personalities involved and the circumstances of their marriage. Such marriages are often entered into hastily after short acquaintance and without due consideration of the realities which must be faced later. An impetuous decision on this most important human relation is always a poor foundation for marriage no matter at what age it may be made.

No doubt many marriages are based on a hasty decision. Some very likely do marry to escape unhappy home situations. The growing youth at times rebels against a continuation of parental authority. On the other hand parents sometimes cannot understand their near grown sons and daughters. In consequence conditions may develop at home which will force a young person into a hasty and ill-advised marriage. Sometimes conditions outside the home, such as loneliness or dissatisfaction with school, may provoke a hasty marriage. Whatever

Escaping unhappy home   Loneliness

Social inferiority   Sudden impulse

FIG. 6. MARRIAGE UNDER PRESSURE

It is a great hazard to hurry into marriage because
of pressure from any source.

may be the pressure conditions, a marriage to escape an
intolerable situation is a foolish venture. Marriage does
not come first in the consideration, as it should, but the
primary consideration is given to the intolerable conditions which one desires to escape; marriage is simply a
secondary matter, and that is not worthy of the institution
or of the two whose lives are involved.

Social inferiority may be the occasion of a hasty marriage. A sudden wave of popularity may be very dangerous to one who has not known it before. In such a situation an opportunity for marriage may be quickly and
foolishly accepted because it is the first chance. On the
other hand some make an ill-advised decision to marry
because they think it is the last chance.

More often perhaps the foolish marriage is entered into without thinking at all. The reasoning processes are not exercised. The two simply drift along into this momentous experience without giving a serious thought to it. No attention is given to the maturity needed, to the meaning of marriage, to the similarity of interests so necessary for success, or to the mutual determination to live together congenially which should be basic in this mature enterprise.

Too often the hasty marriage results from a sudden impulse. One is overwhelmed by a compelling urge to stake all of his life on a fling. With reckless abandon he suddenly throws himself into marriage. Although marriage is a venture of faith and mutual trust, its entry demands a much larger exercise of mature human personality and judgment than is expended in a sudden sweeping impulse.

A decision of this magnitude should be made calmly. It should be based upon good judgment. No undue pressure from any quarter should force a person into it. Only such a calm and unhurried decision befits this weighty matter of marriage.

IV. At What Age Will You Marry?

You expect to be married someday. It is a sort of hazy expectation. The haziness should lift as you apply your intelligence to this interesting matter. Forethought should be given now to the right age for marriage so that you will have a rather well defined idea of the maturity you expect to attain before marriage.

1. *When You Are Full-grown*

Physically you will expect to be full-grown. You will not want to undertake the responsibilities of marriage until you have achieved the full stature of adulthood. Very few grown people are limited in marrying by physical handicaps. If you are mature in stature, have good health, and are not crippled from illness or congenital deformity, you have requisite physical maturity for marriage.

(1) *What the law says.*—The laws of the land require that you shall have reached a minimum age before you can marry without parental consent. The minimum legal age varies according to the laws of the different states. In most states it is twenty-one years for the man and eighteen for the woman, although some states require the woman also to be twenty-one. Georgia has the lowest age requirements of seventeen and eighteen. With parental consent the minimum legal age for marriage is some years younger. A number of states also recognize common law marriage, or marriage without legal license or ceremony, but such a marriage is hardly likely to concern anyone who will read this book.

(2) *"Marriage in the sight of God."*—This is a commonly heard expression. It is used in two ways, sometimes to apply to a couple who have not yet married, of whom it is said that they are already "married in the sight of God" because of their intent to marry and their genuine devotion to each other; it is also used sometimes to refer to uncongenial couples who have been legally married, but of whom it is said that they were never really married "in the sight of God" because of the absence of the genuine devotion which ought always to mark marriage. Each is a foolish and mischievous statement. Marriage, although ordained of God, becomes a reality through an accomplished fact of human experience. Marriage in the sight of God is no different from marriage in the sight of man. A man and woman are married because they have united their lives, they live together as husband and wife, their

union begun in civilized society on the basis of a legal license and a civil or religious ceremony. It is silly to say that a courting couple who plan soon to be married are already married in the sight of God as much as they ever will be or that another couple who are legally married are not married in the sight of God because of their incompatibility. In either case marriage is or is not an actuality, depending on an accomplished fact; it has no reference to any relation "in the sight of God" apart from the joining of two lives together. You will be married when you link your life with another "for better or for worse, until death do you part." Public signification will be given to it by legal license and public ceremony; you are *not* married before, either in the sight of men or in the sight of God, and you *will be* ever thereafter.

(3) *A few years beyond twenty.*—All of the conditioning factors which have influenced your life have prepared you to wait for this event until you are of the normal chronological age—about twenty-five for men and twenty-two for women. Your family's attitude will have real bearing on the exact age at which you marry. Your own judgment as it relates to your own circumstances will determine the exact date. Prior to this normal age for marriage you will know that you have not attained the maturity necessary to make a wise decision. For instance, your ideas on the sort of wife or husband desired will change as much after you are sixteen as they will on the matter of vocation. You will realize that you are not ready for such a momentous decision even in your late teens. A few years of experience beyond twenty will give you a much better basis for such a choice.

2. *Economic Maturity*

Economically you should have attained some maturity. How much money should the groom have in the bank on his wedding day? This is always a lively question for a group of young men. Young women too are not lacking in interest. In one group of young men, the author recalls, several suggested $250, others held out for $500, and one even suggested $1,000. Another group of men and women thought that there ought to be $4,000 in the bank before the wedding and that a $4,000 salary would be adequate. The amount one thinks that it is best that he should have for marriage usually does not coincide with the actual facts when he marries. The author remembers quite distinctly that he had the sum of $50 which he had borrowed from a brother.

Those who have studied the facts say that there is little if any correlation between the size of income and marital happiness. In general, they report, there is no difference in the amount of marital happiness among the well-to-do, the average, and the poor. They do insist that a man should have established the fact that he can earn a living. Such can be demonstrated, it is pointed out, only by a successful work record. It is suggested that one should have used his vocational knowledge in making a living for a period of not less than one year.

(1) *Firm grasp of economic principles.*—More important than the amount of one's resources or even than his work record, is a firm grasp of fundamental economic principles—of industry, of frugality, and above all, of honesty. The young couple who understand that they are to earn their livelihood through constructive, diligent endeavor in worth-while employment, that there are no short cuts to riches, that they are to spend only that which they earn, and that they are to save from the outset a part of each month's salary will make an economic success of their marriage partnership.

(2) *The wife's contribution.*—The wife's contribution to the economic well-being of this partnership needs

special attention. Her special and distinctive economic function is usually in the area of management. In some cases she will add to the family exchequer through employment, but in every case she will handle a major part of the family expenditures. As purchasing agent, especially of grocery and household items needed daily, she will largely determine whether the family income is spent wisely or foolishly, frugally or extravagantly. Both wife and husband will also prove their economic maturity by their ability to suppress a desire for things until they are able to buy them.

(3) *Christian stewardship—a sound policy.*—There is another most important principle in economics which is omitted entirely by the secular writers in this field and many times is neglected by young people at marriage because of expediency. This is the principle of Christian stewardship. One is not mature economically as a Christian until he realizes that the best investment he can make with his money is that which he contributes to Christian work. Tithes and offerings are better investments than any stocks or bonds. Tithing is a sound economic principle. You will be on safe ground economically if you enter marriage well grounded in and guided by the Christian doctrine of stewardship.

(4) *Character of occupation.*—Increased income does not always bring increased marital happiness, the studies show. More important is the character of one's occupation. It should provide regularity of work and income and should be marked by a high degree of social control and by little mobility. For instance, schoolteachers who must answer to the community rank high in marital happiness. Of course, intelligence and favorable personality factors are a part of the answer, but the regularity of their work, the social supervision given to it, and their relative permanence of residence do loom large in the explana-

tion. It is significant that unskilled laborers and traveling salesmen, who move more than any other groups, are rated lowest in marital happiness.

3. *After Graduation*

Educational maturity is another important qualification for marriage. All studies show that happiness in marriage is achieved in direct relation to education. In general, those with higher education make a better success of marriage. It is also true that those with higher education usually marry later. One cannot be certain whether it is the education and the delay that have the helpful effect on marriage or the quality of the persons involved. High type persons usually are ambitious to secure the best education that can be had. Their success in marriage may be but a reflection of the type of persons they are and not altogether because of their education.

Formal education is preparation society gives to the young to equip them for adult responsibilities. Marriage marks full entry into adulthood. Most, if not all, of your years in school should be over before you marry. This does not mean that you will cease to be a student—not at all—or that you will cease your intellectual growth. It will be the exceptional case when formal education is continued very long beyond marriage.

4. *Spiritual Maturity*

Spiritual maturity is also a requisite for the responsibilities of marriage. A rational person before reaching adulthood will come to a clear position concerning God, concerning himself, and concerning his relation to God. A solid outlook of faith concerning life—its origin, its mission, its destiny—and unswerving trust in God are most needful equipment for marriage.

Religion needs to be shared in the home. The husband-wife relationship will become more beautiful day by day if a common faith draws them together. In your quest of a marriage partner you will do well to find one who shares your faith.

5. *Emotional Maturity*

Emotional maturity is important. Marriage is an affectional relation. It is based on the strong feelings of two people for each other. It is a venture rooted characteristically in the emotions. Most important, therefore, is this matter of emotional maturity.

The range of emotional development is traced in detail in chapter V but here it may be noted that when emotional maturity is achieved, one is able to direct his affection to one person in a singlehearted devotion. He offers and receives a pledge of devotion to which he will be true for life. He has singled out one person as the object of his undying love. He is mature emotionally.

That is the type and degree of maturity most needed for marriage. A couple should be full-grown emotionally before they set their wedding date.

SOME THINGS TO THINK ABOUT

1. What factors determine maturity?
2. How does spiritual growth reflect itself in daily conduct?
3. Do you think age difference is important in marriage?
4. What are the causes of hasty marriages?
5. Which is more important for happiness in marriage, frugality or a well-paying job? Honesty or a large bank account?
6. Is tithing a sound economic policy for newlyweds?

Chapter IV

Signposts to Success

Can two walk together, except they be agreed?
—AMOS 3:3.

Final success, then, is not a matter of what you start with, but of your attitude toward the whole process of living together.—PAUL POPENOE.[1]

One day you expect to marry. There are a great many things about this approaching event of which you are not now certain. You probably do not know the date and you may not even know the person who will join you at the altar. But there is one thing of which you are certain.

You are sure that your marriage will be a success. You know that you want to succeed here more than you want to succeed in any other direction. More than you want wealth or position, more than you want fame or fortune, you want your home to be stable, peaceful, and a source of high joys. You want your marriage to be marked by all of those qualities which would cause you to call it a success. Success anywhere and everywhere else turns to ashes in one's hands if he fails in the daily living of his own home.

What are the signposts to success in marriage?

The one general rule for success, or happiness, or congeniality in marriage is similarity. People are attracted to each other because of similar viewpoints, backgrounds,

[1]Paul Popenoe, *Modern Marriage* (New York: Macmillan, 1946), p. 32.

attitudes, personalities. They get married on the basis of similarities. Their happiness in marriage, scientific studies prove conclusively, is in direct relation to their points of similarity.

I. FAMILY BACKGROUND

This principle of similarity applies to family background. Married couples usually come from similar family backgrounds, and success in marriage is experienced most often by husbands and wives whose own families have marked similarities. In general, then, similarity of family background is prophetic of success in marriage. This is the general rule. Specifically you will want to compare the economic life, the social status, the moral standards, the religious affiliation, and the health of your two families. Other matters regarding family background also need careful attention.

1. *Attitude Toward Family*

First is the matter of attitude toward one's family. If one is happily related to his own family, getting along well with his parents and brothers and sisters, it is very likely that he will succeed also in the new relation of his own home. But if one does not get along well with his own family there is reason to believe that the present difficulties may be re-enacted after he marries. If a boy is sullen with his father, he will likely display this same temperament toward his wife. If a girl is hateful to her mother, she will later show the same mean streak to her husband. If one flies into a rage at his brothers and sisters, he very likely will do the same toward his husband or wife or children. The wedding ceremony works no quick miracles in human personality. One carries the same faults and foibles into his new relation.

2. *Are Parents Happily Married?*

Are his or her parents happily married? Happiness begets happiness, and a child who grows up in a happy home is likely to be a good marriage risk. On the other hand, if there is unhappiness between parents it may indicate a serious personality or character default which may be passed on to the child by heredity or by environment. Moreover, the child who grows up in a home with unhappy and poorly adjusted parents may have adopted

FIG. 7. PRODUCT OF A HAPPY HOME

One who grows up in a happy home will very likely build a happy home.

a defeatist attitude which is fatal to marriage. Some children growing up in such a setting will profit from their parents' mistakes and will give themselves more diligently to making a success in marriage. What such a situation does to a person's chances of happiness in marriage depends on the person and how he reacts to these experiences.

3. *Is He Tied to Mother's Apron Strings?*

A parent fixation is another very serious possibility. The child may be attached to his father, or his mother, to the point that no one else can come first in his affections. Most often it involves mother and son. It grows out of the mother's inability to allow her son to grow to maturity. In consequence she dominates his life. His every decision is dictated by "what Mom would think." A girl marrying such a person thinks that she has married a man but finds to her sorrow that she has adopted a grown baby who wants to be mothered. Any type of parent fixation—mother-son, father-son, mother-daughter, father-daughter—can have devastating effects on marriage. It is a possibility which needs to be examined most carefully and weighed accurately if found to exist.

4. *Are There Clinging Relatives?*

Danger lurks in the possibility of clinging relatives—a parent or brother or sister attached like a leech to husband or wife. Certainly every person faces a duty to parents and blood relatives which must be discharged else one is recreant to an inescapable duty. One contemplating marriage with another would certainly be cautious if there has been a flagrant failure to discharge such a responsibility to his first family; such a record would be prophetic of a similar attitude to be displayed later toward the new home which he proposes to establish. On the other hand, if there are clinging relatives, happiness in marriage can be severely tested by these members of the family who are always on one's doorstep. Either extreme is to be avoided.

II. Religious Viewpoint

The highest good in human existence, the Christian will quickly assert, comes through a definite acceptance of Christ as Saviour and a day by day walk with him. Christ in one's heart and life enriches, ennobles, enlightens as no other experience possible to man. Christ in the home can make of it a very heaven on earth—the richest and finest state in human relations. Christian marriage between two who are definitely Christian and who live the spirit of Christ daily is the very finest and best marriage relation.

For marriage, as affected by religion, the principle again is congeniality. If religious views, no matter what they are, are shared in the home there is less likelihood of conflict. Sharing of religion makes for harmony in the home, especially in the training of children.

1. *Congeniality Is Possible in Mixed Marriage*

Two people of different denominational affiliation may live together happily without serious conflict, depending on the degree of difference in their religious viewpoints. The effect of difference in church affiliation on any mixed marriage will depend on how ardently each holds to his views.

Consider the two religious views which are farthest apart—the Catholic and the Baptist. One, the Catholic, says that salvation is in the Church and that men are to be saved only by coming within the fold and submitting to the authority of the Church; the other, the Baptist, says that salvation is in a person, Christ Jesus the Son of God, and that one is to be saved by individual, direct approach to him through faith, which trust alone is the human requirement for receiving God's free grace offered through his Son. These are extreme views and if held sincerely by two could be the basis for serious conflict within the marriage bond. And yet it is possible that a Catholic and a Baptist may live together happily in marriage.

It depends on the Catholic and the Baptist. Suppose, for instance, that the Catholic is a nominal one only. He was brought up in the Catholic Church. He has been confirmed. He takes the sacraments. He knows that the Catholic Church assumes absolute power over the human soul for time and eternity. He is aware that his church teaches that all other Christian denominations preach heresy and that their adherents are doomed for hell. But he listens to this arrogant doctrine with an inward smile. He views Rome's blandishments of her awful power with tongue in cheek. He simply does not believe that an ecclesiastical system headed by a human despot in the Vatican City actually wields the power over human souls which it claims for itself. He believes that every person must approach God individually for himself without the hindering factor of some human intermediary. He is a Catholic in name only and not in fact. He may indeed be a New Testament Christian in spite of the awful error by which his church holds millions in bondage. He may meet another New Testament Christian—a Baptist—on common ground, and their marriage may be marked by religious harmony in their home.

But the reverse may be true also without conflict and the result may be a peaceful home. The Baptist may be one in name only. He may feel that his church should exercise full authority over his immortal spirit. Thus as a nominal Baptist there may be no fundamental conflict between his views and those of his Catholic companion. There may be congeniality of religious viewpoint in such a case which will make for happiness in marriage. If congeniality of faith does exist between a Baptist and a Catholic, it will be because one or the other has never accepted the fundamental doctrine of his church.

The interfaith marriage most hazardous, according to the studies in this field, is the one between the Jew and the Catholic. Next is that between a Protestant or evangelical and a Catholic, while the third most dangerous is between the Protestant and Jew.

2. *Beware of Marriage to a Catholic*

Special attention needs to be given to marriage between a Catholic and Baptist or Protestant. The Catholic, if he is consistent, accepts the authority of his church.

FIG. 8. CATHOLIC-BAPTIST MARRIAGE IS MOST HAZARDOUS

The Catholic accepts the authority of his church. He flouts it at the risk of his eternal destiny.

The Baptist accepts the authority of the Book. Individual responsibility is the principal belief.

That authority is more binding than anything else in his life. He flouts it at the risk of his eternal destiny. That dread authority has spoken very definitely concerning any contemplated marriage to one who is a member of a so-called "schismatic" or "heretical" sect (which in Catholic terminology simply means a Baptist, a Presbyterian, a Methodist, or some other evangelical). On the the other hand, the unwary lovelorn Baptist or Protestant has no such authority on which he can rest; even in marriage he is at liberty to marry not only whom he pleases but when and where and how he pleases. No church law is binding upon him with respect to marriage.

What laws of his church govern the Catholic? First, he must be married by his church. No other marriage, civil or religious, is valid to the Catholic. If I were a Catholic, I would simply be married by a Catholic priest. So would you. Else, in my mind, my marriage would not be valid, I would be living in adultery, and my children would be born out of wedlock. The Catholic who is a Catholic indeed must be married by his priest. Any other marriage would do unspeakable violence to his conscience and would give rise to such fears as the human spirit could never endure.

Second, the Catholic party to such a marriage in private conference with his priest must agree to do everything within his power to bring his mate into the Catholic church. He must also pledge that the children will be brought up in the Catholic Church.

Third, the Catholic may receive a special dispensation to marry a non-Catholic only on condition that the non-Catholic sign an agreement in the presence of the priest. In it the non-Catholic promises:[2]

---

[2]Quoted from p. 4, "To Sign or Not to Sign" by F. E. Mayer, Concordia Publishing House, St. Louis. This leaflet on the Catholic pre-nuptial contract is available from Baptist Book Stores for seven cents.

1. that I will not interfere in the least with the free exercise of the Catholic party's religion;

2. that I will adhere to the doctrine of the sacred indissolubility of the marriage bond, so that I cannot contract a second marriage while my consort is still alive, even though a civil divorce may have been obtained;

3. that all the children, both boys and girls, that may be born of this union shall be baptized and educated solely in the faith of the Roman Catholic Church, even in the event of the death of my Catholic consort . . .;

4. that I will lead a married life in conformity with the teachings of the Catholic Church regarding birth control, realizing fully the attitude of the Catholic Church in this regard;

5. that no other marriage ceremony shall take place before or after this ceremony by the Catholic priest.

Thus through this contract does the Catholic Church extend its strong arm not only into the new home which is being established but beyond into the lives of unborn generations. Thus does the Roman Church preclude the possibility of congeniality of religious viewpoint in the marriage relation between one who is a consistent Catholic and another who is a consistent New Testament Christian of some other denomination.

As intolerant as the Catholic Church is in this matter, it should be kept clear that Rome is wholly within her rights and is frankly consistent with her fundamental doctrines in this matter. Rome boldly proclaims that all others are in error and that theirs alone is the true Christian church. Such narrow dogma demands Catholicism's intolerable practices in reference to marriage. The consistent Catholic has no alternative except to subscribe to these demands. He must be married by the Church. He must bring his children up in the Church or else, he believes, they will be damned. He cannot flout the authority of the Church at any point without peril to his eternal salvation.

John and Mary think that they can overcome this obstacle. They love each other devotedly. John agrees to sign the contract, but tells Mary frankly that he does not mean to abide by its terms. They go to the priest and John repeats a similar statement with more force.

"I am signing this contract," he says to the priest, "simply because you require it and Mary will not marry me unless I do. I do not intend to keep its terms. I am practicing your doctrine of mental reservation. We will bring up our children on a fifty-fifty basis. I'll take the children to the Baptist church on one Sunday and Mary can take them to hers on the next."

What happens? John and Mary are married. John insists on a rigid observance of the fifty-fifty rule. After a dozen years their eldest, who has attended Baptist services half of the Sundays and Catholic services the other half, makes a profession of faith in the father's Baptist church. Mary is obdurate. No child of hers will ever be baptized in a Baptist church—at least not until she is eighteen when she can do as she pleases. Thus the inevitable conflict continues between two who are devoted to each other. They wrestle with a problem for which there is no solution as long as each holds consistently to his belief. The child also is brought into this ceaseless conflict between his parents.

A Protestant-Catholic courtship poses an intolerable dilemma: the surrender either of the fiance or religious convictions. Any possibility of religious harmony is ruled out by the conditions imposed by the Roman Catholics.

3. *Beware of Marriage to a Follower of Alexander Campbell*

A certain Methodist married a girl who was a member of the Church of Christ. She and her family persistently insisted that he unite with her church by baptism. If he did not, they said, he would surely go to hell. One can understand the basis of such an insistence when he realizes that they sincerely believed that the man was doomed if he did not submit to their baptism.

"They nearly worried me to death," the man relates. "Finally, I told them that my mother and father were good people, that I believe they were Christians even though they were Methodists. 'Both,' I said, 'are dead and gone. I believe that they are in heaven. If they are not, I am willing to go to hell with them. Now shut up, and quit bothering me about your Campbellite baptism.'"

This actual experience illustrates the tenacity of the followers of Alexander Campbell. When such a view is held by one member of a marriage partnership and is expressed repeatedly, it can become a most irksome circumstance. The very name which Campbell's followers have adopted—the Church of Christ—implies an assumed monopoly which makes for intolerance. In fact both in attitude and in possible effect on marriage there is a strong parallel between Catholicism and Campbellism. Each sets up an ecclesiastical system through which it is claimed that God's grace is available only at their hands, the one offering salvation through baptism and the other adding six other sacraments and imposing its complete sovereignty over the trembling individual. Both inculcate an intolerance which in effect practically obviates the possibility of happy marriage to one of any other faith.

4. *Beware of Marriage to Any Religious Zealot*

There are a number of other sects well known for their zeal—Jehovah's Witnesses, Mormons, Christian Scientists, Nazarenes, Adventists, the Assembly of God, etc. An overwhelming zeal, of course, may also mark a Baptist or a Methodist or a Presbyterian. Zeal for the cause of

Christ is a great quality, but an overwhelming passion which amounts to fanaticism may spell danger for marriage, especially if you do not share the religious fervor and viewpoint of the zealot.

It is the sharing of views which makes for harmony in marriage. Especially does the sharing of faith make for concord and tranquility in the home. Dissimilarity of religion in any form may spell disaster.

III. CULTURAL BACKGROUND

Suppose you—a young man—live in Arizona where there are 113 marriageable men for every 100 marriageable women. You discover that in South Carolina there are nearly twice as many women as there are men. Will you quickly make your way to South Carolina to find a wife? Probably not, and the little matter of expense will not be the only factor. You realize that a belle from old Charleston might not be entirely congenial with ranch life under Arizona's bright skies.

Again suppose that you—a young lady of Mississippi— decide that your matrimonial opportunity lies in Wyoming where there are 142 marriageable men to every 100 marriageable women compared to the ratio of only 56 to 100 in your native Mississippi. Will you hie yourself to the west in search of a cowboy? Again the matter of difference in cultural background is a paramount factor. You are not sure that your upbringing in the deep South fits you for marriage to one who has roamed the Rockies.

You want a companion in marriage who speaks your language, who shares your customs, who appreciates your viewpoints. In short, you want one whom you can understand and who understands you. Such understanding in marriage is most likely when two come out of similar cultural backgrounds.

Of course, intercultural marriages to a degree are taking place constantly. In the normal interplay of life young people are meeting from different communities and from diverse cultural settings. In such normal associations it is to be expected that marriages will result. War, bringing together young people from across the world, results in extreme cases of intercultural marriage many of which end unhappily simply because of the wide difference in cultural background.

If you and the one you marry have a similar cultural background you have another reason for assurance that your marriage will be a happy one.

IV. Similar Education

The rule of similarity for success in marriage applies also to education, with one interesting exception. The records show that people usually marry in general those who are on the same plane from the standpoint both of educational attainments and intelligence. The records also show that marriages between people of similar education are most likely to succeed.

The interesting exception is that the husband may surpass the wife both in training and in intelligence without drastic peril. The reverse, that is where the wife excels her husband intellectually, is most hazardous. This circumstance grows out of the apparent innate masculine desire to dominate and the complementary feminine willingness to acquiesce in such dominance.

A young wife writing to Dorothy Dix could not understand why her husband objected to her enrolment in night school. She had had more years of formal training than he had. They were happy in every way except at this point of the wife's desire to take night classes which came on nights when he was away from home at his work. He was simply furious about it. She was bewildered and hurt. "Why can't I have four hours of my own to do as I please each week?" she sobbed.

Evidently this girl did not understand what was back of her problem. She did not realize that the male of the species cannot endure feminine superiority. Intellectual equality he may accept but superiority, never. Bright young women if they would enhance their chances of marriage should either seek the company of those who are as bright or brighter or else appear to be dumb!

V. ECONOMIC STABILITY

A marriage gives promise of succeeding happily for both parties if they share like economic views. Happiness in marriage is not conditioned upon wealth, although poverty may be grueling and abject want can bring real misery. Two industrious young people who have a grasp of the fundamentals of economics need not know want in this land.

1. *The Fundamentals*

The very first principle of economics has to do with satisfaction in worth-while work. It is through constructive and socially meaningful labor that men provide for themselves the physical necessities—the so-called consumers' goods of our American way of life. And yet in America with its definite socialistic trends there is danger that young people may be slow in learning this fundamental economic concept. For instance, government—municipal, state, and federal—is employing increasingly larger proportions of the working population. But government produces none of those manufactured articles which all of us want. Increasingly more of our population are turning aside from the constructive employment which produces a sound economy. All of

which may contribute to a failure on the part of young
people to grasp the good satisfactions from work. If a
young couple work because they get joy out of working,
because they know it is honest, because they realize they
are helping to produce consumers' goods which the world
needs, they are on safe ground.

The second economic principle is conservation. That
which God gives and men make must not be wasted. It
is a sin to waste God's good gifts. It is a crime to squan-
der that which man has manufactured. It is a vice to
destroy one's handiwork. A recognition and acceptance
of the law of conservation is a good economic policy in
the home.

The third economic principle is the application of
good judgment. Materials are to be used according to
the rules. One is to invest his resources not by chance
nor on a hunch but according to the best intelligence he
can apply in the light of every discoverable factor.

2. *Division of Labor*

Now there is in marriage traditionally and of necessity
a division of labor. Failure to recognize it or rebellion
against it can bring great sorrow. A family must have a
breadwinner—one who goes out into the marts of trade
and into the areas of industry to give himself to honest
constructive toil by which he earns substance for
himself and his family. A home must have someone
back by the stuff at the focal point of the family—an expert in nutrition who understands the remarkable chem-
istry of the human body and is able to prepare meals
to meet the needs of the household; a student of the
sciences of textiles and fashions, competent thereby to
select and to keep in order clothing for those she loves;
and, still more significant, a patient, guiding teacher
whose skill is equal to the challenge of growing young

personalities and is able to bring them up in the nurture and admonition of the Lord. Human society simply demands different patterns of work activity. Man by nature and tradition is suited to the spectacular employment out in the world; he can engage in the spurts of activity by which financial rewards are gained. The woman by nature and tradition is apt at the gentler task of homebuilding, child training—the remarkable career of the housewife. In any partnership there must be a division of labor, a recognition on the part of each partner of the lines of duty each will pursue. Such an understanding is of great importance in marriage partnership.

Traditionally the man still represents to his wife strength and protection. She assumes his name, she looks to him for support, he gives to her security. Not every man can be a two-hundred pound athlete at will. Not every man can be a millionaire. Nor is either the type of security the wife needs. But every man can be dependable, stable, honest, trustworthy. That is the sort of economic security needed in marriage—worth far more than either brawn or gold.

VI. Personality

You like to be with a friendly, happy, considerate, optimistic person. Everyone does. No one is happy in companionship with a grouchy, ill-tempered, suspicious, mean individual. Your marriage will have a strong point in its favor if both you and your companion have pleasant dispositions, attractive personalities.

Adams and Packard in their book *How to Pick a Mate* devote five chapters to a discussion of personality in marriage. These chapters include a listing of the "Crucial Traits for a Happy Marriage," a series of tests by which you may measure both yourself and the friend in whom

you are interested, and a second series of tests designed
to reveal how your personalities would match as a couple.

In marriage the significant point is how your personality matches with that of another. Adams and Packard
conclude in their helpful discussion that it is important
for a couple to be alike in most personality traits.

VII. CHARACTER

More important than personality is the basic ground-
work of life, character. Personality is the incidental behavior in normal social contacts which gives a person
individuality. Character runs deeper into the current of
life itself. It refers to the integrity by which one's life
holds together. If you and your friend are true in
character, if you are honest, if your lives are clean, if
your attitudes are wholesome, if your lives are pure and
ring true at every point, you may be assured of happiness
in marriage.

The marriage vow demands that each bring to the
altar a record of perfect chastity, no misstep marking the
life of either, and each giving himself to the other in
perfect fidelity. Monogamy in marriage and monogamy
in morality are but two sides of the same social necessity.
In marriage each gives himself to the other in complete
purity and utmost fidelity.

It is not surprising that the pull of the world is toward
loose moral thinking and loose living. The human spirit
itself is bent on evil. Every popular medium to influence
life plays on human weakness. The movies, the radio,
the magazines find an eager audience as they play on
human lust. The battle for purity of thought and deed
rages within each heart and mind and will. The battle
for morality must be joined in every heart. The dan-
gers of petting and other indiscreet behavior are very
real, and must be avoided with steadfast purpose, for

such activity can build up a cumulative physical desire against which successful resistance is most difficult. The victory will be won and the enemy vanquished within your own soul as you realize that yours is no unusual struggle but is such as is "common to man" and that God will with the temptation also "provide a way of escape." A clean life—clean all the way through—is the way toward success in marriage.

There are two other great vices which threaten the physical, the moral, and the family well-being of America. One is a poison, the rotten brew from decaying vegetation to which men fall prey as they seek an escape and to which they become addicts with fearful toll. You are playing with fire if you are thinking of marrying a person who imbibes liquor to any degree.

The second is a fire more literally—"fire on one end and fool on the other" as has been said often but now with less conviction than in former years. The danger from this fire is the greater because the social conscience and intelligence have been benumbed to its influence. In the popular mind little if any thought is given to the damage done to the human body, crown of God's handiwork and temple of the Holy Spirit, from the poison drawn into one's respiratory system from burning leaves. Yet the intelligent Christian must face the certain fact of tobacco's harm to the body. You may have to face the fact of damage from this weed to the body of one you love. Regardless of what the social attitude may be, it still is true that nicotine is one of the most potent poisons known to man.[3] One cigarette contains enough of it to kill a man.

---

[3] For a full discussion of the harmful effects of smoking see the free tract "I'm Glad I'm Free," by John D. Freeman, published by the Baptist Sunday School Board, Nashville, Tenn., and *What About Smoking?* by C. Aubrey Hearn (Columbus, Ohio: School and College Service, 1949).

Medical science long ago concluded that cancer of the mouth, the throat, and the lungs is often directly related to the use of tobacco. Men of medicine also know that the function of the blood is to take up the poison which is brought into the lungs through smoking. They know too that nicotine-laden blood in the mother is certainly of no advantage to the child, either before or after birth. Tobacco from the standpoint of expense in money and in health is a factor which the wise young person will consider as having relation to his marriage.

Character which issues in cleanliness of life looms large as a sign on the highway to happiness in marriage.

VIII. A REALISTIC APPROACH

In spite of all you do to find a person who measures up ideally every way, when you actually come to marriage the person who stands by your side at the altar will be just another human being filled with faults and foibles. In spite of your every effort to become everything that you want to be, you yourself will still not reach the mark in perfect personality and character toward which you strive. You think that girl you are courting is wonderful and that she has no faults. The fact is, she has her failings just like the next person. You see her only at her best. She is not practicing any deliberate subterfuge, but she does want you to see her when she has on her best clothes and her best manners.

In like manner, you, young lady, think that that young man is the perfect hero—strong, handsome, magnificent in every way. You see him at his best too, but remember that he also has his failings.

So you will be just as careful as you can in reaching this momentous decision of life. But even as you reach it you should realize that the person you are marrying will be another flesh and blood individual. Many people perhaps never marry because they are not able to approach marriage realistically. They cannot adjust their ideals for marriage to the actual human possibilities around them. This adjustment must be made if you are to marry happily and if it is to be a success. For after marriage you must still keep in mind that the wedding ceremony worked no miracle either in the personality or in the character of the one who said with you "I do." He is still human. And you will love him and be true to him in spite of every fault. That is the drive toward getting along, the determination to build a real compatibility, the diliberate effort to be congenial which makes for success in marriage.

SOME THINGS TO THINK ABOUT

1. What aspects of family background are of chief consequence to marriage?
2. What are the possible day-by-day effects on family life of mixed marriage?
3. What elements enter into cultural background?
4. Do young people generally have a grasp of economic fundamentals?
5. On what basis should the division of labor between husband and wife be made?
6. Do you really expect your husband (wife) to be perfect?

Chapter V

Two Hearts As One

Love suffereth long, and is kind; love envieth not; love vaunteth not itself, is not puffed up, doth not behave itself unseemly, seeketh not its own, is not provoked, taketh not account of evil; rejoiceth not in unrighteousness, but rejoiceth with the truth; beareth all things, believeth all things, hopeth all things, endureth all things. Love never faileth: but whether there be prophecies, they shall be done away; whether there be tongues, they shall cease; whether there be knowledge, it shall be done away . . . But now abideth faith, hope, love, these three; and the greatest of these is love.—1 CORINTHIANS 13:4-8, 13 ASV.

Greater love hath no man than this, that a man lay down his life for his friends.—JOHN 15:13.

Nothing is more important for normal marital happiness than the ability to give and receive love. —MEYER F. NIMKOFF.[1]

One of the dramatic developments in the wake of World War II was thrust upon the attention of the nation through the advertisement of a veteran. In the days of battle he had fallen in love with a girl across the seas. Now many months later and separated from her by the wide expanse of ocean, their two hearts pined for each

---

[1]Meyer F. Nimkoff, *Marriage and the Family* (New York: Houghton Mifflin, 1947), p. 344.

other with an unceasing longing. Finally in desperation the former soldier advertised an eye for sale in order to provide the money needed to bring his sweatheart across the ocean so that she might become his bride.

Quickly it was proved again that "all the world loves a lover." The boy did not have to sell his eye. Interested friends, some of them unknown to the lad himself, provided the money and soon the girl had come across the Atlantic. The whole nation was thrilled by this evidence of love which would prompt a young man to offer his eye rather than endure separation from the one he loved.

That is the sort of love which every young lover purposes to offer to his beloved. It is the noble altruism characteristic of idealistic youth approaching marriage. It illustrates the abandon with which a young couple give themselves to each other and lay claim each upon the other in the initiation of marriage. This is the view of love at the beginning.

Let's get a glimpse of love at the end, after two have walked together through life's long way. You have seen it often in a fine old couple celebrating their fiftieth wedding anniversary. There is character in their faces. There is devotion in their glances. They are steadfast to each other, as true as the light. They have known the joys, the anxieties, the sorrows. They have taken life as it has come, together, and it has been a good life because their affection for each other has been true.

Several years ago the author was driving with his family just beyond the outskirts of Atlanta. He was not lost and yet he did not know exactly where he was. Seeing an old man leaning heavily on his cane by the roadside, he stopped the car to make inquiry of him.

"Where does this road go?" the author asked.

With a twinkle in his eye he gave a long "spiel" to the effect that the road led to a certain pike which in turn led to another and it in turn led to the king's highway and "the king's highway will lead you to Londontown."

Captivated by his instant and contagious merriment the author repeated his question to receive the identical reply.

"Well, where are we now?" the author asked.

"You are eleven miles southeast of Atlanta," said the old man, his eyes still twinkling, "and if you follow that road it will lead you to Lithonia and then beyond to the king's highway, for all roads lead to Londontown."

Then fixing his kindly gaze upon the occupants of the car, the old man added sincerely, "Come over and see us sometime. Our house burned down in March and we are making out in a little shanty, but we would be glad to see you. My wife likes company."

The old man had an attentive audience. He told how his mother had escaped from Atlanta ahead of Sherman's marching men. With vivid memory he spoke of the courage of his mother as she snatched him in her arms and led the other children to safety. He remembered how they lived on sweet potatoes for several weeks in their retreat near Savannah.

"Come over and see us," he urged again. "Our little shack is not much, but my wife would be glad to see you."

On and on the old fellow talked. Finally the author and his family had to drive away. Even as they were about to leave he said again:

"Come over and see us sometime. My wife would be glad to see you." Then almost in an undertone, too low for the author to hear him, the author's wife caught his last words: "If you knew her as I do you would love her too."

The poet Robert Burns describes ripened love with eloquent pen in the poem, "John Anderson My Jo." It is a soliloquy of an elderly wife to her companion of the years, "my jo," or my sweetheart.

"John Anderson my jo, John" she says in her quaint speech, "we clamb the hill thegither."

> "And monie a cantie day, John,
>   We've had wi'ane anither:
> Now we maun totter down, John,
>   But hand in hand we'll go,
> And sleep thegither at the foot,
>   John Anderson my jo."

I. THAT'S WHY PEOPLE MARRY

When you marry it will be for love. That is the reason most people in our country get married. In some instances it may appear that economic or social or physical considerations are the determining factors, but in most cases people marry because they think they have found and have given the affection which they want and need.

Genuine affection is both assertive and submissive. It is a receiving and a giving. One claims another for himself and at the same time gives himself to the other. The giving must be more pronounced than the receiving, for otherwise it would be a selfish exploitation of another to satisfy one's personal desires. Real love places the happiness of the beloved above one's own and causes the lover to make deliberate efforts to promote the happiness of his beloved.

It was pointed out in chapter II that Christian marriage is monogamous. The very nature of genuine love requires monogamy. Someone has said that the heart of man is not big enough to love more than one woman.

With singlehearted devotion a true lover must give himself unreservedly and exclusively to another. He does so not selfishly—not to claim another for himself—but to give himself completely to the other in a lifetime of fidelity to one person whom he has singled out as the object of his true devotion for a lifetime.

Genuine affection is progressive. There is a solidity about the devotion of a couple who have been married twenty-five years wholly unknown to two who have just become engaged. The full flowered love of two on their fiftieth anniversary has grown far beyond the first blossoming fragrance which they knew on their honeymoon. And yet there is in prophecy in the early experiences the promise of that which is to come. The discerning young couple who have been drawn to each other recognize their mutual devotion even in its infancy as genuine. They know that it must grow through cultivation and that the ripening fruit of affection will develop according to the attention which they give it.

1. *That's What People Need Most*

Nimkoff in his comprehensive text *Marriage and the Family* tells how tests reveal that infants one to two years old are attracted more by the noise of a spoon clattering on a plate than they are by human voice. By the third week there is a tie in the response to these two sounds. By the fourth week the turn is definite to a more ready response to the human voice which now is linked with deep-seated satisfactions associated with food, warmth, and affection. Already there has been developed a consciousness of the importance of other persons in one's life and the four-weeks-old infant makes a deliberate bid for their favor.

The first object of the baby's love is his mother if she is good to him. This is the beginning of affectional development which is climaxed and given mature direction in marriage. It is also prophetic of one of the greatest continuing needs of the human spirit.

The capacity for love is the superlative human quality. The ability to give and to receive affection is the greatest human accomplishment. It is also the fulfilment of the deepest human need.

Those who are happy in marriage have not only learned how to get along with each other, but they have achieved the highest stage in emotional development. They have a capacity for love. They can give and receive affection.

As we shall see in chapter 7, the great continuing function of the family is affectional. In large measure institutional functions formerly performed by the family have been taken over by other agencies. For instance, education, religious training, and recreation have each to more or less degree been lifted out of the home and made a function of social institutions other than the family. But never can the home be supplanted at the point of the great personality need for affection. Companionship between husband and wife, parents and children meets the deep need of all which no other agency can even fill.

It is remarkable how the meeting of this need lifts one out of himself and causes him to radiate with new attractiveness. "All the world loves a lover" because a lover is lovely. No longer are his interests focused in self. He directs his attentions with abandon to another. The unconscious effect on his countenance and his personality is to bring a new sparkle, a new attractiveness, a new radiance. It does something to one's whole being to fall in love.

2. *Some Never Make It*

For one reason or another, some people go through life without knowing the experience of a singlehearted affectional commitment to another person. Our records in chapter 1 show that about 10 per cent of the population never get married. Many deliberately decide against marriage. With some it is because of a lack of opportunity. The range of possibilities has not been sufficient to provide a suitable mate. With others it is because of rigid and inflexible standards which they are unwilling to adjust in line with the human possibilities. In other instances, timidity may prevent some from making the normal social contacts which would lead ultimately to courtship and marriage. Again selfishness may prevent some from making the full commitment to another which is basic in marriage. Others have had their emotional development arrested by one cause or another and simply can never achieve the maturity of monogamous affection. Others have limited views on marriage and see only the economic or the social or some other personal gain to be derived therefrom and thus never marry because they fail to find one who will give them the advantage in marriage which they seek.

There is no doubt a great deal of unhappiness in the experience of many who go through life without ever knowing the maturity of affection which culminates in marriage.

Some who never marry, of course, accomplish real sublimation of inherent human need at this point. They devote themselves to a cause or they may lavish their affection on a close relative or even on a friend. Lives need not be empty outside marriage nor need they necessarily be unhappy, even though it is true generally that married love offers the highest good known in human relations.

But there is a more miserable state than that of the lonely hearts who are deprived of lasting affection. Far worse is the portion of those who marry but do so on the basis of a counterfeit love.

II. BEWARE OF BOGUS ROMANCE

The greatest damage in marriage is done by what Paul Popenoe in his book *Modern Marriage* calls "Bogus Romance." This modern romantic complex, done up in Hollywood trappings, is portrayed to millions of Americans every week at the movie houses—grown people in an infantile manner playing at what ought to be the most mature experience of human activity, making a mockery of monogamous, permanent, Christian marriage. It is glamorized in a thousand and one secular publications. It is dramatized over radio. It is no wonder that the wreckage of Bogus Romance is heralded by the newspapers every day.

1. *The Counterfeit Pattern*

With discerning and devastating pen Popenoe describes the pattern of Bogus Romance which is doing such damage to American marriage today. First, according to this popular notion promoted by the movie moguls, there is a sudden visitation. One is walking down the street thinking about some deep philosophical subject or pressing world problem. He rounds a corner and there she is. He never saw her before. He does not know her name. Really these little details are insignificant, for this is IT. He has been gripped by a sudden overpowering visitation. A moment ago the visitation was not on. Indeed it was the farthest thing from his mind. But now it is on. It fills him and thrills him and conquers him. That is how love comes, so these

Fig. 9. Five False Planks in Bogus Romance Platform

First, a sudden sweeping visitation

Second, forsaking everything to pursue IT

Third, the visitation may leave as suddenly as it came

But wait! you may have a succession of visitations

Finally, Bogus Romance is an infantile love of self

who preach this silly doctrine believe—suddenly, instantaneously, overpoweringly.

Second, this visitation is so meaningful that one should forsake all to pursue it. He may have vocational plans.

Give them up, if need be, he is counseled by Bogus Romance advocates. One is a sissy if he does not. A man is justified in giving up his parents. If he happens to have a wife and children, he is justified in giving them up to pursue this wonderful visitation which has come upon him. A king is justified in giving up his kingdom. Such is the second plank in this platform of Bogus Romance claiming the attention of the popular mind today.

Third, this visitation may leave as suddenly as it comes. One may turn and walk around that corner in the opposite direction. Now IT is all over and there is nothing one can do to retrieve IT. One had as well be philosophical about it all. IT was great as long as it lasted, but now the visitation is over and one can continue his way thinking about the problems of the world or about questions of philosophy.

But wait, there is hope! For the fourth plank in this amazing platform is that one may have a succession of visitations. One may walk around that corner again and in the right direction. Once more here she is. Again her name, her background, her character, her personality—all of these are of little or no consequence. One is gripped again by a sudden visitation. One may have any number of such visitations, each as meaningful as the other, according to this doctrine proclaimed by your latest movie star whose many marriages were publicized in yesterday's newspaper and whose version of marriage was thrown on the screen in the latest release from Hollywood.

That is Bogus Romance. It is the popular doctrine of the world. But it makes no appeal to the solid intelligence of a Christian young person like you. For in truth it is bogus. It is false all the way through. There is nothing genuine about it. It offers nothing of the solid grip on real affection which must be the basis for lasting companionship in marriage. It is, as Popenoe points out in the final plank, nothing more than an infantile love of self. It is the immature questing of a grown-up infant seeking a sensation. For in each successive visitation the thing that matters is what each of these charmers does to you—the thrill, the sensation that you get from it. There is nothing more than that to it: simply a spurious physical attraction which goes as quickly as it comes, leaving nothing but the empty shell of a passing infatuation of a bogus romance.

This is the false doctrine against which young people must be warned. Every medium which influences thought today is shot through and through with this false doctrine. But such a program is not for the building of a life together. Bogus Romance can lead only to heartache, to disappointment, to ruin, even as is demonstrated in the careers of the playboys who are its most zealous advocates.

Be warned, my young friend. Beware with all diligence of every plank in the platform of bogus romance.

2. "Love at First Sight"

Every friendship has its point of origin. There was a moment when two friends first met and all their contacts thereafter are built on that initial meeting. In like manner every love affair has to have a first meeting. It is possible that there may be a strong interest manifested on that first meeting which develops into real love and results in happy marriage, but most first meetings do not so result and are soon forgotten. It is the spectacular, the unusual case which develops into what is called "love at first sight."

Such a concept could have no other basis except physical attraction, unless it should be a desperate anxiety which prompts a person to take the first available one who comes along.

When two people are so madly in love that they must marry at once, which is often the case in so-called "love at first sight," it is probably infatuation they are experiencing rather than genuine love. Love can wait, but infatuation cannot. Infatuation may die out abruptly, even as it has developed suddenly. It is that fear on the part of those who are thus anxious to plunge into marriage at once which explains their urgency. Deep within themselves they doubt that they have the requisite qualities in themselves and in their experience which will guarantee lasting affection.

Love is not a trap you fall into, either at first sight or at second sight. It involves respect and comradeship which can be developed only from similar tastes, ideals, and yearnings. It cannot result from only one date.

III. Love's Sure Sign

What is love? How does one get it? How can one detect it when it is genuine? Only about one in six or seven "love affairs" leads to the altar. How can one be sure that this is the "right" affair?

Love is an interest characterized by devotion to another's welfare. "To care for someone" expresses well the true sentiment in affection. The focus is upon the beloved one's needs and wishes and not upon one's own. It is not something which can be spontaneously generated or turned on and off at will. The immature, who subscribe to the Bogus Romance doctrine, say that anyone can fall in love. Of course, he must be careful that it is the right person, the one who surely is waiting for him somewhere. But when he finds that person their love for each other is all that matters.   Love, these say, conquers all—age differences, differences of religion, of wealth, of education, poor health, parents' objections, and any other obstacles.   Many adolescents dote on this sort of romance as children do on fairy tales.

1. *Urge Toward Romance Is Strong*

Nimkoff tells about a sophomore girl in college who was asked to express her feelings freely.   The medium used was fingerprint paints on paper.   The girl painted a picture of a flower strewn path on which walked a boy and girl hand in hand toward a cottage at the top of a hill.

She gave expression to a wish common to all.   The conscious desire for love is strong; the unconscious may be even more compulsive.

2. *Affection Needs Rational Basis*

And yet the capacity for love is not instinctive. Young people—and older people too—do not know how to make love by intuition.   Sometimes people go through life with the floodgates kept tightly closed.   They never know how to love or to practice courtship.   Some of them are most unhappy because of it.

Some have their emotional development so twisted by early experiences that they can never relate themselves normally to a person of the opposite sex.   You need to understand therefore the normal steps in emotional development.

3. *Steps to Mature Affection*

The normal person goes through five steps leading to emotional maturity.   These steps began with the beginning of life itself, in babyhood.

(1) *The infant loves self.*—First, the infant loves himself. He becomes aware of himself. He bumps into his crib and discovers his hands, his feet, his head. He soon learns that he can wield quite a bit of power in his own interest by making a peculiar noise with his lungs and vocal cords. He resorts to such a device at all hours—even at three o'clock in the morning, and even though both parents may be dog tired. People say, "That's all you can expect of him. He's just a baby."

And he is excused as long as he is a baby. But he will not be socially accepted for long if he continues to behave like a baby when he is six or twenty-six. Some people seem never to grow beyond this first stage in emotional development. They love themselves only. They have tantrums if things do not go to suit them. They pout and fuss and cry until they get their own way.

Love of self is retained through life, but one needs to lift the horizon of his affectional development beyond self if he is to become a good risk in marriage. It is too bad if a girl marries a two hundred pound athlete and finds to her sorrow that he loves no one but himself. It is too bad if a young man marries a beautiful young woman who is still so selfish as never to have advanced beyond infancy emotionally.

Most people learn early to be considerate of others and to become adjusted socialized persons.

(2) *The baby loves his parents.*—The second step in emotional development is reached when the baby lifts the horizon of his affection in a warm response to the parent, usually the mother. His mother cares for him and is good to him. The baby develops normally an affectional interest.

Again this quality is retained through life, for every normal person loves his parents as long as the parents live. It is too bad, though, if emotional development is arrested at this point. A wife may find it a little embarrassing, for instance, if her husband of thirty-six wants only someone to mother him. Indeed, she will

FIG. 10. STEPS TO EMOTIONALLY MATURITY

The infant loves himself

The child loves his parents

Teeners love their gang

General interest in opposite sex

A man loves one woman

probably be quite vexed if she learns that her husband's attachment to his mother is so complete and exclusive as to make it impossible for him to love his wife in a singlehearted devotion.

Love of parents is normal, but it is only the second step in emotional development. As each stage is reached the widening of the affectional horizon loosens to a degree the ties that bound one to his former associates. Love for parents lessens the baby's love for self, and the further stages of emotional development make less binding the ties to one's parents.

It is possible that even this second stage of love for parents may not be developed. The parent may not be good to the child. Even the mother may mistreat her baby. In such a case the child is thrown back upon himself and his normal emotional development is arrested. The scientists say that he becomes narcissistic. He is self-centered. His normal affectional growth has been blocked. In the same manner there may be a fixation of affection at any stage before one reaches the final platform of emotional maturity. If such a fixation does develop he is unable to direct a deep affection to another.

(3) *Teeners love their gang.*—The third stage is reached when the gang spirit predominates. Boys like to be together, but they despise sissy girls. Girls want to be with one another, but they hate ugly old boys.

This gang age is a normal emotional stage. Its influence is retained through life, but one's emotional development ought not be stopped at this point. If it is stopped, the man will go through life a "woman hater" and the woman a "man hater." Each gets pleasure only in association with those of his own sex. Now as long as one lives he will find pleasure in friendships of the gang type, of his own sex. Men want to be in men's

clubs.   Women like the society of women at teas and
club meetings. It is a normal and natural development,
but it is only the third stage along the way to emotional
maturity.

(4) *Youth loves everyone.*—Fourth, the growing
young person is attracted to everyone of the opposite
sex generally. Again, let it be fully understood that this
is normal but it does not yet mark maturity of affection.
At this point the boy becomes girl crazy. Anyone in a
dress sets him atingle. It doesn't make any particular
difference which girl it is, just so he is in company with
someone feminine.   Girls too may become boy crazy.
One is as good as another. Just anyone in trousers will
do.

It is too bad for marriage if one has not grown beyond
this stage, if one knows nothing more than a general
interest in everyone of the opposite sex.   Evidently
many of the so-called stars of the screen have never
advanced beyond this stage.

(5) *A man loves one woman.*—The fifth stage of full
emotional maturity is reached when one can direct his
affection to another and can give and receive a pledge
of lasting devotion.

Such a mature love is described by Paul when in
Ephesians he admonishes husbands to love their wives
"even as Christ loved the church and gave himself for it"
and wives to submit themselves unto their own husbands
"as unto the Lord." Such a love is the only safe basis for
marriage, for Paul concludes, "For this cause shall a
man leave his father and mother, and shall be joined
unto his wife, and they two shall be one flesh" (Eph.
5:31).

Only one type of human love surpasses the true devotion between husband and wife, and that is the love
of a believer for his Saviour, Christ Jesus.

Dr. Ellis A. Fuller, president of the Southern Baptist Theological Seminary, has told from the pulpit about asking his wife to marry him. Since he has related such a tender scene in preaching, the author makes bold to repeat it here.

"I am not asking you to take the first place in my heart," said the young lover. "I am asking you to take the second place. The first place is reserved for the One who died on the cross for me."

She accepted his love and returned it in kind, knowing that she had received a pledge which could be a safe basis for enduring marriage.

SOME THINGS TO THINK ABOUT

1. Do you think that genuine affection is progressive?
2. In your opinion, how prevalent is Bogus Romance?
3. Is love a trap that you fall into?
4. Is each of the steps leading to emotional maturity a normal development?

Chapter VI

How to Go About It

Politeness is to do and say the kindest thing in the kindest way.—An old spelling book.

And Jacob served seven years for Rachel; and they seemed unto him but a few days, for the love he had to her.—Genesis 29:20.

Elizabeth at twenty-six lives with her father on the farm. Her mother died when she was young. Elizabeth has always helped her father make a living and has kept house for him. She dropped out of high school before graduating. She is in good health but "can't make friends easily" and is "not very pretty." Elizabeth wants boy friends. Her highest ambition is to have a Christian home. So far she has never had the chance to date. She wonders if she should go into some big city to find work. She needs and wants work, but even more she wants "the right kind of friends." Could she find them in the city?

Bernard presents a similar problem. He is thirty-five years old. He frankly wants to know "how to start and successfully complete a true Christian romance." He admits that for a number of years he has been busy at other things. Now he wants to have "love, romance, and glamour of the Christian kind, of course, and win for myself a wife."

Are these isolated cases? If they provoke a ripple of merriment, it may be because Elizabeth and Bernard have been frank to reveal a common aspiration which you are hesitant to express.

I. A Common Aspiration

When one sets out in romantic quest, he is fulfilling a desire common to every heart. He may be certain that the person of his interest shares his own desire for dating, courtship, and marriage—at the right time, in the right manner, and to the right person. This aspiration is so universal that many have fallen into the error of thinking that love making is a skill intuitively possessed. The evidence of Elizabeth and Bernard prove that such an assumption is without validity.

Actually, do young people know intuitively the answers to these heart questions? Do you know instinctively *whom* to love? Do you know *where* and *when* and *how* to meet him? Do you know how to win his interest? Do you know instinctively the fine points of human relationship that will make your courtship successful? Are you certain that you can ultimately bring to the altar the one person you will want to marry?

1. *Two Common Illusions*

Elizabeth, the farm girl, vainly thinks that if she could go to some big city her problem would be solved. There, she believes, the prospects would be numerous, the young men would be attractive, the pickings would be easy. Bernard still pays tribute to the fiction that love making requires some dramatic formula, some sort of spectacular approach known only by the initiated.

Here are the two favorite illusions. One is the notion that the grass is greener in some other pasture—just any pasture except one's own. The second is that success in affairs of the heart can come only through some strange procedure.

2. *The Magic Secret*

There *is* a wonderful formula. But there is nothing strange about it. Many miss it altogether because of its very simplicity. And it never fails. It is guaranteed to bring success, always. Here it is:

If you want to win friends, you must be a friend.
If you want to gain the interest of another, you must show interest in him.
If you want to be loved, you must love.

For if you are to succeed in matters of the heart, you must lift yourself out of the narrow confines of self and direct your attention to others. Only the friend can win friends. And friendliness is nothing other than a genuinely expressed interest in others. Only one who has the capacity for sympathy, for tenderness, for compassion, for unselfishness—in short, the capacity for love—can win and hold the affection of another. For it is the very essence of love to give oneself in utter abandon to another.

This chapter could be comprehended in a single pointed suggestion: Read Dale Carnegie's *How to Win Friends and Influence People* and practice the obvious but profound rules which he elaborates. With some warmth Carnegie declares that the purpose of his volume will be fulfilled if it develops in the reader an increased tendency to think always of the other person's point of view.

Again this chapter could be written in a single sentence:

Greater love hath no man than this, that a man lay down his life for his friends.—John 15:13.

In winning the affection of another the lover does not claim the beloved for himself, but he gives himself to his beloved.

3. *Three Basic Questions*

As you approach this matter of social contacts, dating, courtship, and ultimate marriage, three fundamental questions will recur in your mind and heart. First, What kind of person do you want to marry? Second, Where will you find the right one? Third, How can you win the one you want?

The first question is objective. It has to do with the type of person you want. The second deals with the practical problem of meeting people who measure up to your standards. The third is more important, for it involves the type of person you are. Here is the area for improvement. This is the realm where you can do more about it. It is the place where you ought to work the hardest.

II. WHAT KIND DO YOU WANT?

The kind of friends you have depends upon the kind of person you are. Your personality, your character, your ideals, your interests, your standards, your attitudes are all conditioning factors both in your selection of friends and in their selection of you.

In marriage you will want to make the best match possible. The qualities you seek will be your own standards for a marriage partner evolved according to your own ideals in personality and character.

1. *The Woman a Man Wants*

The writer of Proverbs (chap. 31) lists six superb qualities of the ideal wife. First is moral purity, named in the announced subject, "a virtuous woman." Second is stability: "the heart of her husband doth safely trust in her." Third, she is marked by energy, is no lazy slacker: "She . . . worketh willingly with her hands."

Next, her marketing is based on good economy (vv. 16, 18). Fifth, she has a magnanimous spirit: "She stretcheth out her hand to the poor." Finally, she is sagacious: "She openeth her mouth with wisdom." Such a woman is a benediction to her husband and to her family.

Paul Popenoe, in his wide experience as director of the American Institute of Family Relations, has concluded that there are six qualities which the wise young man will want to find in the woman he would wed. Popenoe discusses these six attributes in his very useful book *Modern Marriage*.

(1) *Her parents are happily married.*—A faulty family background, as Popenoe points out, may develop a faulty personality, although it is possible that the child may profit by the handicap. More significant is the possibility that members of a broken home may be inferior people in every way, the breakup in the home being but a symptom of deeper maladies in the family. "Whether you like it or not," Popenoe adds, "you *are* marrying the whole family, and you will therefore do well to look them over."[1]

(2) *She gets along well with her own family.*—The girl who hates her mother and is ashamed of her father may adopt the same attitude toward you later.

(3) *She has definite interests in life.*—Much family trouble develops because the wife resents her role in the family (of home management and child nurture) and has few if any other interests. Popenoe believes that proper education should prepare girls to get more satisfaction from homemaking and at the same time to enter into community life.

(4) *She has a "good disposition."*—One who is normally happy will be happy in marriage, but one who is

[1]Popenoe, *op. cit.*, pp. 21-29.

selfish, demanding, domineering, petulant, snobbish, dishonest, mean in little ways, or given to sulking and to pouting or to tantrums is not likely to be happy anywhere.

(5) *She should be fond of children.*—The normal person wants a family.

(6) *She should be "typically feminine."*—The qualities Popenoe has in mind are "good grooming, sympathy, gentleness, modesty, grace, refinement, companionability, social intelligence, and responsiveness."[2] To this list should be added the most important quality of all— a definite Christian experience and devotion to Christ.

2. The Kind of Man a Woman Wants

Popenoe says there are three qualities the average young woman hopes to find in the man she marries.[3]

(1) *Strength.*—From of old woman has looked to man for protection. She has even had to entrust her life to the man she marries. This necessity of getting a husband able to take good care of her is the background of feminine attraction to strength and power. Primarily it stands for dependability and protection. You cannot, as Popenoe makes clear, become an athlete or a bank president at will—nor is that the sort of strength which your wife will need most of all—but you "*can* attain financial honesty and dependability, emotional maturity, and moral worth."[3] That sort of strength far surpasses in value a rugged physique or a big bank balance.

(2) *Comradeship.*—Popenoe insists that a man "must study a girl's nature; learn the things that appeal to her; treat her feminine peculiarities with interested respect,

---

[2]*Ibid.,* p. 29.
[3]*Ibid.,* pp. 48-56.

rather than amused tolerance or contempt; and maintain a sense of humor *with* her, not at her expense."[4]

(3) *Romance.*—"Every woman," says Popenoe, "expects that the man of her choice will satisfy her need of a lovelife."[5] Specifically this need will require that young men give "more attention to grooming, to etiquette, to social convention and so-called cultural interests."[6] Popenoe reports a widespread complaint among some girls that many "otherwise superior young men not only lack, polish, but even lack cleanliness."[7]   This third trait he sums up in the word "tenderness."

Again, of course, you will add to Popenoe's list the most important element of Christian experience and commitment.   Most of all, a Christian young woman will want for a husband a man who is a positive Christian.

III. Where Will You Find the Right One?

Elizabeth's question, "Where can I meet the right kind of people?" is one being raised by many young persons.   To Elizabeth, "the right kind of people" means eligible young men.   She thinks that there are none in the farm community where she lives.   She thinks that she could meet them in some big city.

Let's examine that illusion a little more carefully. Actually, according to the statistics, there are more men than women in rural areas.   The reverse is true in the cities. Elizabeth doesn't know these statistical facts.

Nor does she know that it is very difficult to meet people in a city compared to the relative ease of meeting them in rural areas.   She doesn't know that, once the

---

[4]*Ibid.*, p. 52.
[5]*Ibid.*, p. 54.
[6]*Ibid.*, p. 55.
[7]*Ibid.*, p. 55.

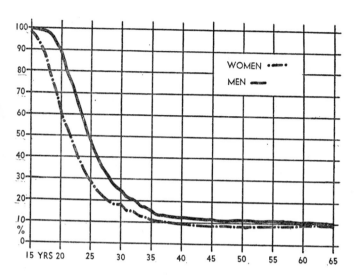

FIG. 11. PERCENTAGE OF POPULATION SINGLE, 1940
This shows the percentage of men and women who
were single in 1940, at specified ages. Bureau of
the Census, *Population—Special Reports* (Nov. 21,
1945).

hurdle of meeting has been crossed, suitable places
and occasions for courtship in the city are scarce. She
doesn't know that in the city public chaperonage in
home, church, and community such as prevails in a rural
setting is practically unknown. She doesn't know that
in the city a young couple may date for many months
and still remain practically strangers to each other.

Elizabeth wants to go to the city, her object being—
although she would not express it quite so bluntly—to
find a man. If she ever finds one, it will be right in the
environment in which she lives and in a manner which

sparks a mutual interest between two congenial personalities. When you "find the right person" it will be
right where you are in the very circle in which you
move.

1. *These Four Succeeded*

I asked four young married people where they had met
their mates.

Lucille, then a high school senior, first met Lonnie
on a hayride. She noted that he was handsome, had an
attractive personality, and that all the girls liked him. He
rated high. A few weeks later she was pleased when he
asked her for a date. Twenty months later they stood
at the altar together.

Edwin was a police reporter on a morning paper.
His duties took him every night to the city hospital to
interview low characters who had been involved in
shooting scrapes and other violations of the law. There
at the desk receiving incoming patients sat Edwina,
smiling, alert, attractive. Edwin liked his assignment
better at once. They saw each other every night. Soon
he was taking her home from work. In nine months
they were married.

Wilma saw the tall smiling visitor at Training Union.
At the fellowship period she chatted with Willard in a
friendly manner because he was a stranger. A few
Sundays later he asked to take her home. Within a
year they set up a home together.

James knew Jewel in a casual way during their first
year at school together. Not until midterm of the
second year did he decide to ask her for their first date.
Two years later he went to see her in the town where
she was working and asked another question. Their
marriage was set for the following August.

2. *It's Always That Way*

There is nothing unusual about any one of these casual meetings. Indeed each case was quite usual, although the young people involved think that it was all very wonderful!

You will find your "one and only" in the same place— right where you live. You live there and move in that circle because of all of the factors that make you the person that you are—your background, your interests, your aspirations, your beliefs. You like people who share

FIG. 12. RATIO OF FEMALES TO MALES, 15 YEARS OLD AND OVER, 1940

States	Females per 100 Males
District of Columbia	110.9
Massachusetts	107.8
Rhode Island	106.3
Georgia	105.9
South Carolina	105.5
Alabama	104.3
Tennessee	103.5
North Carolina	103.1
Louisiana	103.0
Mississippi	102.7
New York	102.7
Connecticut	102.4
Missouri	102.4
New Jersey	102.2
Florida	102.1
New Hampshire	102.0
Pennsylvania	100.8
Illinois	100.3
Ohio	100.3
Kansas	99.5
Maine	99.5
Maryland	99.4
Indiana	99.2
Texas	99.2
Delaware	98.9
Iowa	98.8
Virginia	98.8
Kentucky	98.4
Arkansas	98.4
Nebraska	98.2
Oklahoma	98.0
Vermont	97.4
Colorado	97.3
California	96.3
Wisconsin	96.0
West Virginia	95.9
Minnesota	95.5
Michigan	94.6
New Mexico	94.0
Oregon	92.9
Utah	92.7
South Dakota	91.9
Arizona	91.4
Washington	90.4
North Dakota	88.4
Idaho	87.1
Montana	84.0
Wyoming	81.9
Nevada	75.1

your interests. You like them because they have similar tastes, background, viewpoints. Your friends are within this range of congeniality. The friend who will mean more than all others will ultimately come from your range of associates, from the circle of your daily activities.

3. *Enlarging the Range of Contacts*

Since the person you will ultimately marry will be someone you know—and not someone a thousand miles away you never heard of—the obvious policy is to enlarge the range of contacts. Wherever you live, in hamlet, town, or city, there are steps you can take to enlarge your social range.

You can enter into organizational activities for young people. The best opportunities, of course, are afforded through church organizations and in the social affairs which they sponsor. In these and in other youth groups in the community your social range will be enlarged as you accept active responsibility on committees and in other posts of duty which throw you with others.

Your social range will be greatly enlarged as you develop a friendly personality. A sincere friendliness will make you welcome both by groups and by individuals. Such a pleasant personality will win friends to you generally and will finally win the one friend who will want to spend his life with you.

Dating as contrasted with courtship may be thought of here as a step in the direction of enlarging one's social range. Casual dating, with no thought of "going steady," has definite values quite apart from any serious thought of marriage. It provides pleasant association of boys and girls with one another. It gives experience and ease in boy-girl relationships—a skill the lack of which may be the one barrier explaining the unmarried state of some otherwise very eligible men and women. Further it gives experience in appraising boy or girl friends so that there is less risk of being swept off one's feet by a first but later bogus love affair.

Going steady too early has definite disadvantages. It provides a limited experience in dating. One runs the risk of an unbalanced involvement, one perhaps fancying that he is in love while the other is not ready for such an attachment. Resulting disillusionment may be damaging. The young person may find himself limited in date possibilities because all of their friends identify the two together. Thus the pressure of their going steady may result in their own misinterpretation of their involvement and an ill-advised marriage.

IV. How Can You Win the One You Want?

Patterns of courtship have varied in different ages and cultures. In prehistoric times the cave man snatched his intended bride by the forelocks and pulled her into his abode. Later, tribesmen made forays to capture their women. Other procedures in more civilized cultures have included wife purchase, marriage through parental arrangement, marriage by lot, and weddings for political purposes.

1. *Jacob Worked for Rachel*

A favorite story is the one about Jacob working fourteen years for Rachel (Gen. 29:9-30). It warms the heart to think on his steadfastness to menial service in order to win the hand of the one he wanted. One is thrilled by the romance suggested in the statement that "they seemed unto him but a few days, for the love he had to her."

Compensation expended for a bride may not be wholly evil. If one works fourteen years for his bride he is likely to have real appreciation for her when he brings her to the altar. Moreover, he is not likely to have a light attitude toward breaking up the marriage if it has really cost him a pretty penny to bring it to pass. Today, alas, some girls are dangerously easy to marry. It requires little if any effort to bring them to the altar. But those of real worth are the most difficult to win. They will not fall for any little whippersnapper who thinks that he can win a lady's hand by the slightest beck and call. The sort of marriage you want will still require initiative, industry, and imagination—not the kind which Jacob expended perhaps but an earnest effort which will make you know that a real payment has been made for the bride won.

Jacob saw Rachel under all sorts of conditions. Their first meeting was at a time and in a place where Rachel least expected to see her future husband. It was at noonday under the stress of a tedious sheep tending task. Jacob lived in the home for fourteen years. They saw each other in times of happiness, disappointment, defeat, victory, discouragement, hope, sorrow, and joy.

2. *Overcoming Ignorance*

The bane of modern marriage is the comparative ignorance on the part of bride and groom of each other. That explains many failures in marriage today. Even though young people may marry after months or even years of dating and courtship, yet they may still be comparative strangers. They have seen each other only under favorable circumstances. On dates each is on his best behavior. Each is wearing a mask, not to deceive, but because it is perfectly normal for one to make a display of his best qualities under such circumstances.

Here are some suggestions to overcome this difficulty: more dating and less early going steady; playing games together; picnics and outings; any activity in a group which involves being together for several hours; serving on committees together; visiting informally and often each in the home of the other. The alert young person will think of other specific projects by which two who have a growing mutual interest may each have an opportunity to study the personality and character of the other under all manner of circumstances. Adults who have the responsibility of planning and directing youth activities must also face frankly this need and address themselves earnestly to the problem in a deliberate effort to help young people today in their social contacts to see each other under varied conditions.

There was ample time for the affair between Jacob and Rachel to mature. Exactly fourteen years! Today some young people feel that economic or vocational or educational circumstances make necessary too long a delay in their wedding plans. Yet it must be remembered that these plans must be geared in with all of the factors of maturity enumerated in chapter 2. If one has gained maturity at one point, he must hold himself in check patiently until he gains maturity at other points. Discipline is a continuing necessity throughout life. It is the person who is mature in every way who can make of marriage the full rounded experience which marriage should be.

3. *Moderns Have Some New Tricks*

Primitive man resorted to capture, abduction, combat, exchange, service, gifts, purchase, persuasion, infant betrothal, arrangements made by parents, tribesmen, or some other go-between. Such methods will not work today. The absence of economic ties in family life shifts the emphasis to companionship and love, the great cohesive factors binding the modern home together. In our

day when the family has relatively few economic and
other institutional functions, romantic love assumes
greater significance as the basis for marriage. The
successful young swain must be adept in the fine skills
of winning affection. His quest grows out of an affectional
bent. He does not go out to buy or to capture but to
win. The accomplishment of such a purpose requires
a thorough understanding of the qualities and techniques
for winning favor. The crude procedures of the past are
passe in favor of the subtler skills of attraction.

4. *When One Is Engaged*

There are reasons for a period of engagement. Its
length will depend on circumstances but in most cases
it need not be long. Unless there are some unusual factors necessitating delay, the marriage may well follow
a few months after the engagement has become definite.

Usually some time is required to make the necessary
plans for marriage and to get personal affairs in order
which need attention before the wedding day. The betrothal period is a well established social custom by
which two young people set themselves apart for each
other.

It affords an apprenticeship in mutual accommodation.
Now that their permanent interest in each other is public knowledge, the young couple will be at greater liberty
to be together and to study and adjust their personalities.
Each will visit more in the home of the other. They will
be together more often and under varied conditions.

The period of engagement enables the partners to mature emotionally. The discipline of a time of waiting
will develop their companionship and the spiritual qualities of their congeniality. Their approaching marriage
will thus become more firmly grounded in lasting ap-

preciation for personal values which make for enduring family life.

It would be a mistake, as Paul Popenoe wisely warns, "to turn betrothal into common law marriage or a mere lark."[8] Successful marriage, he adds, is promoted by recognizing the purpose of the engagement period and using it wisely for that purpose.

V. THESE FOUR SUCCEEDED: A SUMMARY

Again let me refer to Lucille and Lonnie whose romance began on a hayride; to Willard and Wilma who met at Training Union; to police reporter Edwin and the girl at the desk, Edwina; to James and Jewel of the long and cautious courtship. I talked with only four of these, with two of the girls and two of the boys.

Several things I found in common. Their experiences may be somewhat typical.

Each had an interest in the other from the beginning.

Each was friendly to the other in an easy sort of way. Neither was strained or ill at ease in the presence of the other.

Mutual encouragement marked the period of dating and courtship but without any strained or deliberate effort to win the favor of the other. They liked to be together and each encouraged their continued association.

The entire experience practically amounted to a discovery. Each recognized that here was a person of fine character, pleasant disposition, and similar interests. The more they were together the more they wanted to be together, and so they are, always.

---

[8]Popenoe, *op. cit.*, p. 175. His chapter on "The Betrothal Period" is a valuable contribution to a right understanding of engagement.

SOME THINGS TO THINK ABOUT

1. What is the most common illusion in affairs of the heart?
2. How important do you consider family background and relationships in choosing a marriage partner?
3. Where does one usually meet the person he marries?
4. How can one get a true picture of the person in whom he is interested as a basis for a wise marriage choice?

Chapter VII

When Two Strike Out Together

*God setteth the solitary in families (God . . . brings the lonely home.—Moffatt)—*PSALM 68:6.

*Marriage has appeared an atempt at emotional security and personality fulfilment which has made it a human quest unrivalled in both the quantity and quality of its demands. . . . An indispensable function of the family is to provide . . . the certainty of an unchanging affection.—*E. R. GROVES[1].

Your marriage will create a new social unit, the duo-personal relation which from time immemorial has constituted the family. This ever-interesting but ancient institution, antedating history, is primary and fundamental in all social organization. Indeed, it is of such significance as to cause E. R. Groves to say that society depends upon it "Not only for its social soundness but even for its very existence."[2]

I. A HUMAN NECESSITY

Both the meaning and the need of the family, therefore, become well-nigh socially axiomatic. The needs

---

[1]Ernest R. Groves, *The American Family* (Chicago: Lippincott, 1934), pp. 418, 420.

[2]*Ibid.*, p. 443.

met by the family run deep in the current of life. All of the personal elements of self-realization, security, affection and response, aspiration, sympathy, discipline, and accomplishment reach their true values in the family setting.

Life is lived out in the family. Here is the setting for the enactment of the cycle of life: birth, infancy, childhood, youth, adulthood, senility. At every step along the way the vital relations of the home give zest or apathy, misery or joy according to the quality of family living.

1. *Man's Need of the Family*

The only conceivable human experience without the family to which there is any recorded allusion is the brief span immediately after the creation of Adam. That lonely episode was happily terminated by the divine conclusion: "It is not good for the man to be alone." From that day till this God has brought the lonely—men and women and children—home. The fundamental need of the family and its primary personal function are comprehended in the divine decree establishing the family.

Put a person in a social vacuum—without a family, ever, at the beginning of life, in midstream, or in the senile years—and of what have you robbed him? He is limited at once in his capacity to provide for himself sustenance, the daily physical necessities. He is deprived of fellowship. He is cheated of culture, desensitized to the standards of action that win approbation. He is even stunted spiritually, for faith itself is most often quickened by family nurture.

To state these facts is to voice the obvious. If there is an absolute anywhere in all of the realm of human organization, it is found in the home. The family is a human necessity.

2. *Two Together—and There Is No Turning Back*

Marriage in a sense is a declaration of independence. You have separated from your natural family; two streams of life which have fashioned two independent personalities have now come together volitionally to form a new family. The two of are on your own. Sink or swim, live or die, succeed or fail, you must make it together now as independent individuals in partnership living.

And there is no turning back. Life itself is never at a standstill. Each successive stage obviates forever the possibility of any return to an earlier period. When once you have stood before the altar, never again can you be a child in your parents' home. It is a step beyond recall. There is a finality about marriage which forever lifts you out of the relations of earlier years and gives you a new status.

II. Roles in Life

The satisfaction which you and your companion will find in your new family will depend in large measure on the poise, the understanding, the confidence, and the discrimination which mark your assumption of these new positions. Each member occupies his own position in the family by reason of character, personality, and attitudes.

1. *Husband—Wife*

The first relation of the family is that which is solemnized in the exchange of vows at the marriage altar. What is the position of the husband in the home? What is the role of the wife?

Time was when the answer was simple. The husband was the absolute autocrat, ruler of his wife and children.

But the old patriarchy is passing away. Woman's struggle for independence is succeeding nowhere so spectacularly as in the family. Already it has brought a changed woman's status in the home hailed alike by modern husbands and wives. For the old order was distasteful and unchallenging to discerning man, the master, even as it was irksome to woman, the slave.

What then are the respective roles of husband and wife today? There is no easy rule of thumb. There is no single answer. The solution which suits you may not do at all for John and Mary next door who were married last week. John has his own distinct points of personality, and Mary also is just as individualistic as the next bride. The interaction of these two personalities, John and Mary, will define and establish the role of each in their home, just as similar factors will differentiate the roles of husband and wife in your new home.

Suffice it to say then that marriage is moving more and more toward an interpersonal companionship which seeks reciprocity in respect, judgment, emotional balance, and spiritual vitality, as well as in affectional response. It may also be added that the husband and wife roles should be clearly defined in your own mind—not articulated in words necessarily, but demonstrated at the appropriate time by the acceptance of a position and the discharge of its duties in a manner approved by your companion. Even an equalitarian relation such as the modern family is becoming still requires some pronounced differentiations. A partnership of equals demands a mutual acceptance of distinctive duties. There must be a mutually agreed upon division of labor. Who will be the breadwinner? Who will prepare the meals? Who will clean the house? Who will give the patient guidance needed by a tiny new life? These and other questions will be resolved not altogether by any mandate of nature,

FIG. 13. DIVISION OF LABOR IN HOME

Who will be the breadwinner? Who will clean the house? These questions will not be answered by any law, but by two devoted Christians finding their roles within the framework of family fellowship.

nor by any decree of society, but by two interacting, devoted, and intelligent Christian personalities finding their roles within the framework of family fellowship.

2. *Mother-in-law*

There is sometimes a holdover from the natural family which may prove to be a trial to the new home. This is particularly true in the case of a parent fixation or when a parent of one of the newlyweds seeks to compensate for some lack in his own experience by exercising control over the child even after marriage. The mother-in-law role is not an easy one to fill successfully. The difficulties confronted may indeed be more a product of social conditions than the result of personality deficiency on the part of the parent. Our culture demands that the mother give herself with abandon to the child; her very achievement in so doing makes more difficult the necessary relinquishment when the child, now full-grown, comes to marriage.

In some cultures the newly married couple become a part of the home of one of the parents, but in ours success in the undertaking requires that the new home become independent at once. Thus the need psychically and emotionally for separate living quarters, especially one that is separated from either set of parents. This signifies no lessening of affection for parents but simply points out the separate and independent status of the new family unit.

3. *Parent—Child*

Here again the interaction of personalities brings satisfaction according to the degree of mutual respect, understanding, and consideration. The child himself rebels against a coercive family atmosphere not because he is unduly self-willed but because even in his mind the family is regarded as a fellowship which is successful to the degree that it brings satisfaction to every member. In such a fellowship the child's personality is outraged by coercion to the degree that his consciousness of self has developed.

The modern trend toward increased respect for personality as between parent and child does no violence to the traditional roles represented by the maturity of the one and the helplessness of the other. The infant's immaturity still finds its complement in the parents' maturity. The nurture given the child by his parents remains the strongest influence in his life. As long as one lives he never escapes the influence of his home. But the respective roles are not of lordship and servile docility but of patient maturity helping weak steps through devious pathways by understanding, tenderness, and untiring devotion.

III. FAMILY FUNCTIONS

The family as a functioning unit operates in certain areas. These activities or functions may be grouped under four headings: economics, fellowship, personality growth, faith.

1. *Economics*

There are three significant phases of the family's economic function. These are the three necessary activities regarding family sustenance.

(1) *Earning a livelihood.*—Usually the principal breadwinner is the husband. This viewpoint is so completely accepted that a man in our economic organization today will receive greater compensation than will a woman performing the same service.

Sometimes—in increasing number today—the wife works part time or periodically to supplement the family income. In some cases due to unusual circumstances the wife or mother must bear the full financial load. Sometimes the children work to provide part or even all of the family income.

Here is a family necessity. "If any will not work, neither let him eat" (2 Thess. 3:10 ASV) is a scriptural and economic axiom. A living must be earned for husband and wife, for parents and children. Full employment of all able-bodied people in constructive activity is imperative to the economic well-being of the community. Work provides the necessities needed for human comfort, the very sustenance on which life depends. The nonworker is a social parasite. He has no just claim to the food he eats, the clothes he wears, or the shelter over his head. He who by subtlety or by some game of chance or by force of arms seeks to gain his livelihood does wrong in every direction—wrong against God who said "six days shalt thou labor"; wrong against society, for all of us are dependent upon the co-operative labors of all able-bodied persons; wrong against self, undermining character.

Work is a good discipline. Moreover, the Christian finds in work the realization of personality which is in fulfilment of the divinely ordained order. The Christian knows that work is honest and that it is honorable. He recalls that Jesus said, "My father worketh hitherto, and I work." The high standard of living in Christian cultures is in no small degree due to the Christian conception of work.

The traditional division of labor which makes breadwinning a masculine function does not give the husband exclusive rights in his earnings. This principle needs firm establishment in the minds of husbands and wives. The salary check may be drawn in favor of the husband in payment for economic services which he alone renders, but there are other economic services rendered by the wife and children which have real family and even community value and justify their fair claim on the earnings of husband and father. The principle, therefore, of joint and equal sharing in the family income is sound. It is neither wise nor right nor Christian for the husband to regard his salary as his alone. Family well-being will be promoted by the fellowship attitude that all that is earned belongs to all of the family.

(2) *Bargaining.*—The second phase of the family's economic function has to do with use of the available money to meet the family's needs. Here is the application of the principle of equal sharing in family resources.

Someone must know the family's physical needs. Some-

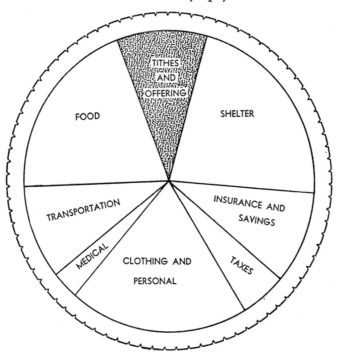

FIG. 14. A FAMILY BUDGET

A budget is a family commitment to keep expenditures within a relative scale. It helps to unify desires and promotes the spirit of industry and sacrifice to reach mutually accepted goals.

one must study merchandise. Someone must know values in fabrics, in food, in furniture. This knowledge based on continuing application to the details of family purchasing is essential if the family is to derive the greatest good from the available means.

Haphazard buying without forethought or planning offers only the prospect of disaster. Installment buying also has real risks, for too often desire, whetted by high-pressure advertising, will goad one to take advantage of credit which exceeds his actual resources. Rigid discipline which holds expenditures within the available means is the only safe fiscal policy for the family. Desire stimulated by advertising and easy credit, if abused, can bring a family to the brink of financial disaster.

There is, no doubt, some real and perhaps widespread rebellion against a family budget because of its disciplinarian aspects. A carefully planned budget is a family commitment to live within the income according to agreed upon relative expenditures. The records which must be kept and the accounting which must be made constitute a discipline against which any spirit of irresponsibility rebels. Of course, no one specific budget will meet the needs of any two families, but the idea of careful planning for wise use of family income is a sound economic procedure.

A budget—or any program of spending—involves proportions. The budget, for instance, specifies the proportion of the family income to be spent for food in relation to the amount to be spent for clothing, or for education and personal advancement. Working out a budget, therefore, becomes a fine family experience in discrimination and assessment of values.

Right at this point is involved the matter of stewardship and the Christian couple's practical application of their own doctrine of financial support to kingdom work. The proportion given to religious purposes reflects the family's long range evaluation of Christian work. So-called contributions are really an investment in values and plainly reveal whether the family holds religion to be dear or cheap. Even a sociologist like Nimkoff is distressed that the average American family contributes only 1 per cent to religious purposes rather than the biblical 10 per cent.[3] He notes with alarm that twice as much is spent for toiletries and other items of personal care, twice as much for tobacco, and ten times as much for the maintenance of an automobile. "Data like these," Nimkoff concludes, "tell us a great deal about the values of American families."[4] The practice of tithing for the Christian is in recognition of the worth in kingdom service rendered thereby—worth to the family, worth to the community, worth to a sinful and needy world. No expenditure in the family budget purchases the values as does the amount given to the Lord's work.

Working on the budget gives unity to the family. It helps to solidify their common interests and aspirations. It gives to the members valuable experience in social enterprise for the common good. It helps to unify desires and promotes the spirit of industry and sacrifice toward the attainment of mutually accepted goals. Some member or members of the family must be expert in certain values, such as in foods or clothing or furniture, but a planned family budget requires unity of decision in the over-all pattern of family spending.

(3) *Preparation.*—The third phase of the family's economic function has to do with the applied use of provisions purchased to meet the family's need. Food must

---

[3]Meyer F. Nimkoff, *Marriage and the Family* (New York: Houghton Mifflin, 1947), p. 725.
[4]*Ibid.,* p. 726.

be prepared. Clothing sometimes must be made and always must be kept in condition for wear. The house's furnishings require daily attention.

The person who is responsible for a family's well-being from the standpoint of food has no little task. Domestic scientists know that food not only controls bodily growth but also that it affects the emotions, temperament, personality, and all of the finely balanced personal responses which point toward contentment or misery. Quantity and quality in food are not enough; balance in diet, proper seasoning, expert cooking, and tasteful serving are added attributes of the family meals done with right regard to the nutritional and associated emotional needs of the home. Mastery of these skills is a worthy accomplishment—worthy enough to warrant lifetime study.

"The way to a man's heart is through his stomach" is more than a truism. It is also the way to health and happiness in the home. There is, no doubt, a great deal of neglect here. Much unhappiness and disease in the home—even death itself at times perhaps—results from want of care in the selection, preparation, and serving of food.

Traditionally this has been a feminine responsibility. The culinary arts are mastered best by those who have peculiar gifts of patience, diligence, and affection. A part of this service can be provided commercially by industry, but the final graceful touches are beyond the reach of impersonal or commercial interest. The profit motive cannot meet the need here. This service in fine and because of the delicate aesthetic values desired, can be rendered best by hands that are tender, out of a heart motivated by love, and from a mind centered on the needs of those who are dear. There are times when the man in the home, due to unusual circumstances, may take over these duties. Indeed the interests of the family are safe-guarded against dire effects of an emergency if he has attained some skill in the kitchen.

The woman's traditional superiority in these matters is a compensating factor operating to the loss of the man left alone. The man without a family may earn the same salary as his office neighbor who has a wife and nine children, but the widower or bachelor can never pur-chase with his increased pro rata earnings the values represented in a meal prepared by tender hands backed by informed intelligence, nor can he with his money pro-vide the tasteful home decorations arranged by loving care.

For the same considerations apply also to the tasteful use of home furnishings and to family clothing. Here again are skills involving family happiness, to the study of which delicate attention is rewarded in happiness and health. The best performance in these areas is accom-plished through applied devotion exercised on the basis of intelligent and diligent study.

2. *Fellowship*

A more significant family function is in the area of com-panionship. This is indicated in the affectional purpose of marriage. When you marry it will be *for* love. The preposition expresses both the causative factor and the goal in view—that is, because of and in order to. When the proper time comes and you have attained the pre-requisite experience—that is, when you are in love—you will marry. Your marriage will be because you are in love. But you want love; you will want it all your life; therefore, you marry. You have it and you want it. It is a realization and an expectation.

(1) *Affection.*—Here is the primary function of the family. It satisfies personal need for affection. The satis-

faction of that need is the one experience which gives security in human relations. That is why E. R. Groves says that the indispensable function of the family is "to provide the child in his earliest years with the certainty of an unchanging affection."[5] But the values operate not alone for the child. For the adult as much as for the infant safety in a highly competitive world is found in the mutual devotion which more than all else defines the successful home. That is the reason, too, that psychologists have discovered that the thing that frightens children the most is to discover that their parents no longer love each other. Of course it does. Their little world has shattered to bits in the wreckage of their parents' lost affection. Nine million children in America have made that frightening discovery.

Their little lives are floundering on the shoals of insecurity because their parents failed to cultivate the fine devotion which they professed at the altar; their homes have been broken on the rack of a dead affection.

Many years ago the author conducted a funeral in a West Texas community. It was the final service for a young mother who left in addition to her sorrowing husband two or three small children. In the friendly custom of the community the neighbors had come into the simple home until they filled the house and were out in the yard, awaiting the announced hour for the service. The author recalls that he was standing just outside the kitchen door by the brokenhearted husband and father—saying little, simply trying to lay his heart alongside the father's in this dark hour. As he stood there he saw a perfectly thrilling sight. The father's little daughter, about five years of age, slipped her hand into

---

[5] E. R. Groves, *op. cit.*, p. 420.

his and almost imperceptibly put a little pressure on his rough fingers. Then just barely above a whisper she said words angels would have rejoiced to have heard.

"Daddy, I love you."

That is the thing that holds a home together. That is the quality the loss of which no home can sustain. A home can survive sickness or financial disaster or even death of one of its dearest members—and indeed such an experience may only solidify the depth of feeling which holds a family together. But a home cannot sustain the loss of affection.

And it is that very quality which the human spirit must have. And give. Somewhere along the way—better, all along the way, every step of it—one must find love. One must love and be loved. Think of the infant in his helplessness and of his utter poverty if he does not feel a heart beating fast for him. Think of the other side of that joint experience—of how much the parent needs the child, of how the strength and devotion of the parent are repaid in the receptive weakness of the child, the need both to love and to be loved met in parent and in child. Marriage itself is but a reassertion of this primary quest to love and be loved. Think then of the deep human values found in the fellowship which brings this quest to realization. Think of the older person in his latter years without a family, to whom his life has meaning for no one. The person without love in his life, be he helpless infant, an adult in the vigor of maturity, or an aged octogenarian, is deprived of that which all need. The family alone is bound together by such ties.

(2) *Assurance.*—The fellowship of affection gives man the only certain assurance he finds in human relations. Everywhere else he is a competitor. Here alone his place is assured because of reciprocal love. But even so his quest is successful progressively, never as a static achieve-

ment. Affection is something which can never be taken
for granted. It must ever be vocal. The affection which
one seeks in marriage and family living, therefore, is an
accomplished fact only with reference to the past; for
the future, it can ever remain an achievement to be attained, a reality to be expressed. One is challenged
always to measure to the degree of fellowship required in
such a personal relation the essence of which is devotion.

(3) *Anchorage.*—Fellowship in the home provides security in a world which is very unstable at every other
point. It also gives anchorage. The English have a song
they like to sing, "East, West, Home's Best." In the
Houses of Parliament after the day's debates are over
the cry is often sounded, "Who goes home?" The answer, of course, is everyone does—statesmen, laborers,
merchant men, children, housewives, all find a point of
anchorage in the fellowship of the family. This tie to
the home has meaning throughout life. One finds himself coming back to his home or its teachings, for practical necessities, for spiritual reinforcement, for every
value to sustain life in the stresses and strains of tem-
pestuous living. The home is an anchor through choice
fellowship based on affection.

This anchorage has utmost value as it applies to moral
and spiritual grounding. God's promise of guidance,
"Thine ears shall hear a word behind thee, saying, This is
the way, walk ye in it," often is fulfilled through the
influence of a Christian home. Fellowship in the family
is an appropriate setting for moral and spiritual guidance
which every life needs. The home has profound influence
in shaping lives along these lines. Verily it is a day when
such moral grounding is sorely needed. Temptations
abound. The pull of the world is toward conformity to a
heedless, pleasure seeking pattern. The steadying influence of Christian homes must save the day.

There is a great deal of criticism of the family today, especially from mental hygienists. The personality problems which they study point back to family failure. The incompetence of parents to provide the sort of fellowship which would save their children from personality defaults has led some of these hygienists to propose that some of the training functions of the family could better be done by experts. They would supplant parents with experts. With all of their boasted proficiency, experts could never supply the needed nurture of a loving fellowship. The family alone can meet the needs for an intimate fellowship.

3. *Personality Growth*

The family is unique also in the congenial setting it provides for the development of personality. It is this function which the family has performed so poorly, according to the mental hygienists. And yet the family, as E. R. Groves points out with clarity in his standard work *The American Family*[6], is operating in the same complex modern environment which has provoked a new examination of the basic structures of government, of economics, of education, and even of religion. He is not surprised, therefore, either that the complex conditions of the day should put unusual strain on the home or that the hygienists should frankly ask for a new evaluation of such a basic institution as the family. The criticism, therefore, serves to focus attention quite sharply on the primary function of the family. It helps clarify particularly the home's range of influence on developing personality.

The family is a close group held together by personal interest. In it there is a constant interaction which has

---

[6]See his chapters "The Mental Hygiene Approach" and "The Successful Family."

profound influence on the development of every personality involved. In each case the development may be
negative or positive according to the character of the
total influences brought to bear by the other members of
the household. What one is, is in large measure the
result of his experiences, and the early, the most forma-
tive, the most powerful influences come from the home.
As Groves says, parents may die, but the home never
passes. Its influence lingers.

The family is unique here. Its influence is subtle. It
influences personality development not consciously but
by reason of feelings, of attitudes, of almost unwitting
interplay of personalities.

4. *Faith*

The fourth family function is in the area of spiritual
development. The family's influence on faith is tremendous. A friend was once described by the unique
statement that he had been "a Virginian for two hundred
years." Similarly, it may be said of some that they have
received Christian influence through many generations;
others, tragically so, have never known the joy of salvation because of the generation-to-generation influence of
forebears.

Religion in the home needs deliberate expression. Here
comes into play the highest form of nurture of which the
Christian home is capable. Every instance of behavior
signifying faith in divine resources is a conditioning factor in the home's influence on the child. It is true,
therefore, that every home has an involuntary religious
influence, for good or for ill, on every member of the
family. Whether the parents will it or not, their conversation and walk in the home before their children will
have spiritual influence, of negative or positive value.
Agnosticism cannot be passive in influence. Jesus' words

FIG. 15. FAMILY RELIGION

The family's influence on faith is tremendous.

ring true with special import in the home: "He that is not with me is against me."

But the deliberate nature of Christian nurture in the home offers the most rewarding field for religious guidance. In daily intimate associations of the family the finest opportunity of all is afforded to bring "children up in the nurture and admonition of the Lord." To a fuller discussion of this highest function of the family the concluding chapter is devoted.

The home deals with life—life in its origin, life in its unfoldment, life in its expression of personality, life in realization, in aspiration—in affection, guidance, development, discipline, restraint, discrimination, evaluation. Life is what it is—good or bad, noble or culpable, heroic or selfish and weak—largely because of the home. The home gives nurture—physical, psychic, emotional, spiritual.

SOME THINGS TO THINK ABOUT

1. Discuss the statement: "The family is a human necessity."
2. Is genuine respect for personality the right basis for defining roles in family life?
3. Is earning a living more important than buying the family necessities or preparing the food and clothes?
4. Do children need the security of affection? Do men and women?
5. Can a home be Christian by accident?

Chapter VIII

Christ's Way in Your Home

> *Except the Lord build the house, they labour in vain that build it.*—PSALM 127:1.
>
> *Therefore whosoever heareth these sayings of mine, and doeth them, I will liken him unto a wise man, which built his house upon a rock: and the rain descended, and the floods came, and the winds blew, and beat upon that house; and it fell not: for it was founded upon a rock.*—MATTHEW 7:24-25.

A Christian home is the goal of every serious young Christian. This aim is so definite as to be practically a truism. And yet the qualities which make a home Christian are perhaps not so clear in our minds. What is a Christian home? is a question often answered in vague generalities. Further, there is similar lack of clarity on the effective steps one may take to make his a Christian home. These are the two important questions claiming our attention in this concluding chapter: What is a Christian home? How can you build a Christian home?

I. WHAT IS A CHRISTIAN HOME?

A Christian home usually is defined in retrospect or in prospect. That is, one thinks of ideal home life in comparison with or in contrast with the home of his childhood, or else he conceives it somewhat vaguely as the wonderful home which he aspires to have. It is an idealization from the past, or a dream for the future.

One or the other of these two views, or more likely a combination of both, will probably fashion your definition of a Christian home just now as you contemplate the establishment of a home of your own.

1. *The Backward Look*

It is normal to look back on childhood experiences with fond recollection. You remember the happy play, the congenial fellowship, the absence of responsibility, the warmth of parental care. Your parents stand for security, tenderness, sympathy. Your parents were to you the rock of strength—strong, dependable, devout. They were to you all that was finest and best. If they had any faults, perhaps you did not even know about them, for always they were to you the soul of care and unselfishness. Your parents and your home mean so much to you that you are likely to define your ideal home—the Christian home—in terms of the family relations of childhood. Even if one's early home was unhappy, he is likely to associate it with what he thinks to be a Christian home by way of contrast; thus he will magnify the faults and failures of his childhood home as being the major points he is determined to avoid in building his own Christian home.

Again, if one's early home was happy, the process of idealization becomes active. He remembers the happy occasions; he forgets the unhappy ones. In his mind, his childhood home becomes perfect, no unfortunate circumstance marring his memory of it. Thus is solidified in his own mind the thought that a Christian home is identical with the home of his childhood.

Now if we begin to list the qualities which marked our childhood home, it is likely that we will not put as much emphasis upon Christian activities as upon Christian spirit. It may be that you never heard Dad lead in public prayer and that Mother never taught a Sunday school class. Your parents may have been so reticent about spiritual things that neither of them ever read the Bible aloud to the family. It may even be that no expression of thanks was given at mealtime. And yet you remember other qualities, and you say that yours was a Christian home. You remember your parents' sturdiness of character. You remember how they gave themselves unselfishly in care of the family. You know that they stood for Christ and his church and for moral principles. Your home was Christian not so much because your parents were forward in expression of their Christianity, either in public or in the family circle, but because of faith evidenced in Christian principles practiced in everyday living.

2. A Look Ahead

As you look toward your home of the future you are determined that yours will be a Christian home. "A Christian home," you will say in your heart, "is what mine will be." It is a goal you expect to attain; it is an ideal toward which you strive.

Really, ten years from now you will no doubt still be striving toward that goal. For a Christian home is always something beyond. It is ever an ideal toward which we work. You might know a home of a mature couple of which you would say that it is truly a Christian home, and yet the father and mother in that home would be the first to deny that their home had become all that they want it to be. In this respect Christian homebuilding will always be a vivid example of the truth of Browning's lines:

"Ah, but a man's reach should exceed his grasp,
  Or what's a heaven for?"

3. *A Platform for a Christian Home*

(1) *Faith in God.*—A first requisite of the Christian home is daily definite reliance upon God. This is shown in the earnest petition which Jesus taught his followers to pray, "Give us this day our daily bread." It is evident by the attitudes and the activities which prove unmistakably that the members of a family believe that God is and that he is a rewarder of them that diligently seek him. They trust not in the deceitfulness of riches, or in the false strength of material things, or yet in their own cleverness. They believe in God.

(2) *Trust in Christ.*—But faith becomes more definite than a mere theistic doctrine, more personal even than reliance upon divine providence. A Christian home is one being built by Christians—people who have definitely committed themselves to Christ for personal salvation. To say that only Christians can build a Christian home seems to be superfluous, and yet there is a growing tendency to use the word Christian in such a broad sense as to rob it of its distinctive meaning. We call ours a Christian America, when, of course, we know that it is not. In like manner we may speak of a Christian community, or even of a Christian home, with little thought of the necessary experience of personal regeneration through faith in Christ by which one becomes a Christian. It is no loose cultural sense in which the word Christian is used here. A Christian home can be built only by people who are Christians—by a husband who has definitely surrendered his heart to Christ and joined by a wife who in like manner has realized the joy of salvation by a commitment of her heart and soul to Jesus Christ as Saviour for time and eternity.

(3) *Mutual love.*—Jesus' new commandment that "ye love one another" applies with particular force in the

Christian family. The Bible says that a man should love his wife even as Christ loved the church, and that a wife should submit herself unto her own husband "as unto the Lord." Children are admonished to honor and to obey their parents. Parents are charged to bring their children up in the nurture and admonition of the Lord. The goal of every member of a Christian family will be to grow in the love which they have one for another.

(4) *Good will.*—A Christian home will cultivate sincere appreciation for people of all racial, cultural, and economic circumstances. The members of the family will seek to show genuine human sympathy toward neighbors, friends, acquaintances, people of every land.

(5) *Christian conduct.*—The Christian knows that he cannot fashion his conduct according to the pattern of the world. A higher standard is demanded. The behavior of members of a Christian family will be marked by daily life *in* the world according to standards which are *above* the world. There will be definite evidence that the members of a Christian home are not conformed to the world, but are transformed to a higher pattern of daily living by following Christ.

(6) *Stability.*—The Christian home holds together because of the character of its members. They have sturdiness. They are dependable. There is certainty in their relation because Christ is in their hearts. The certainty of this relation is guaranteed by their Christian character.

(7) *Church loyalty.*—The Christian family believes in Christian institutions. They are certain that Christ knew what he was about when he established the church. They support the church because they believe it to be fundamental in human affairs, an agency which meets the needs of those of their own dear circle and of all people everywhere. Their loyal support to Christ's cause

through his church is a further expression of the steadfastness of their Christian character.

II. PUTTING CHRIST IN YOUR HOME

As you think of the Christian home which you will have one day, there are three distinct periods which you will need to consider. These have to do with what you can do before you marry, what you can do in your marriage, and what you can do after you marry to make yours a Christian home.

1. *Before You Marry*

First, you will surely seek the Lord's leadership in the choice of a companion. Marriage is an appropriate matter for earnest prayer. You will do well to linger long and often in prayer to God for his guidance in this most important step.

The second consideration is the religious experience of the person you plan to marry. If you are to have a Christian home, you can do so only by being joined in that enterprise by a person who also is definitely a Christian .

Many young people must face this question very earnestly in the days of courtship. That is the time when it should be faced. One should decide beforehand if he is willing to marry an unbeliever. One may have a happy, congenial home with a person of high moral standards who is not a Christian, but can one ever have a definitely Christian home if his companion does not share his sincere commitment to Christ? Many strong young Christians have deliberately turned aside from a friendship which was heading toward courtship at this very point. They have concluded that they would not marry a person who was not a Christian.

Others, deceived by the illusion that marriage will accomplish every desired reform, have plunged into marriage with the vain hope that the marriage partner will soon be won to Christian faith. Of course, that is possible. Christians are all of the time seeking to win unbelievers, and personal and family ties are a motivating factor in much of this effort. Experience has shown that it is rather difficult to reform a husband or wife after marriage. Many have found that it is not easy to win a companion to Christ. One cannot be sure of success; too many have failed, and have gone through life carrying the almost unbearable weight of anxiety for an unbelieving companion's spiritual well-being. If your principal goal is to have a Christian home, you had better be sure first of all that your companion-to-be is a Christian.

Third, if you are to walk together in Christian home-building you will do well to share spiritual experiences and purposes in advance of marriage. In your attendance upon Christian services and in your association together, you will discover in the other the depth of consecration, the spiritual desires concerning your home-to-be, and the general framework of Christian growth as a ground for anticipation of your continued spiritual development together.

2. When You Marry

The wedding of a Christian couple is a significant spiritual experience. Its significance can be heightened by the manner in which it is conducted. The weight of responsibility rests on the minister. In a peculiar way the ceremony is the function of the bride's pastor. He can add a meaning to it by reason of his previous ministry and present responsibilities which no other person can. This is no place to discuss in detail the pastor's ceremony, but the following form will help to indicate its spiritual potentiality:

Dear friends, we are gathered here in the sight of God and in the presence of this company to join these together in holy matrimony, which is an ancient and honorable estate, ordained of God, regulated by his commandments, blessed by our Lord Jesus Christ, and to be held in honor by all men.

Those who enter into this relation are instructed by God's Word each to love the other even as himself, the wife being charged to submit herself unto her husband as unto the Lord, and the husband being directed to love his wife even as Christ loved the church and gave himself for it. For this cause—that is, by reason of this compelling affection which a man and a woman find themselves to share for each other—shall a man leave his father and mother, and shall be joined unto his wife, and they shall be one flesh.

Let us pray.

Our blessed Heavenly Father, whose presence is the happiness of every condition, and whose favor sweetens every relation: we beseech thee to be present with us now and to add thy special favor unto these thy servants, that they may be truly joined in the honorable estate of marriage, in the covenant of God. As thou hast brought them together by thy providence, sanctify them now by thy Spirit, giving them the frame of heart fit for their new estate; and enrich them with all needed grace to enjoy the comforts, undergo the cares, endure the trials, and perform the duties of life together as becometh Christians, under thy heavenly guidance and protection; through our Lord Jesus Christ. Amen.

Now these two, John Doe and Mary Doe, have come hither to be joined in this sacred relationship.

John Doe, will you take Mary Doe to be you wife, to live with her after God's ordinance in the holy bond of marriage, and will you promise in the presence of God and before these witnesses to love her and comfort her, honor and cherish her, in sickness and in health, in prosperity and in adversity, and, forsaking all others, remain faithful to her as long as you both shall live?

John: I do.

Mary Doe, will you take John Doe to be your husband, to live with him after God's ordinance in the holy bond of marriage, and will you promise in the presence of God, and before these witnesses to love him and comfort him, honor and cherish him, in sickness and in health, in prosperity and in adversity, and, forsaking all others, remain faithful to him as long as you both shall live?

Mary: I do.

What tokens do you offer in pledge of your vows?

These rings you will give and receive in token and pledge of your constant faith and abiding love each to the other.

Forasmuch as you have solemnly pledged yourselves to live together in the holy bonds of marriage, and have declared the same before God and this company, I now pronounce you, John Doe and Mary Doe, husband and wife.

"Intreat me not to leave thee, or to return from following after thee: for whither thou goest, I will go; and where thou lodgest, I will lodge; thy people shall be my people, and thy God my God: where thou diest, will I die, and there will I be buried: the Lord do so to me, and more also, if ought but death part thee and me."

Whom God hath joined together let no man put asunder.

Now unto Him that loved us and gave his only Son in our behalf be glory and dominion and power, through our little lives, and through the lives of these who this day have pledged their undying devotion to each other, and beyond even through the little ones who shall come, please God! as a holy benediction into their home, through Jesus Christ our blessed Lord. Amen.

A church wedding adds spiritual warmth and dignity to the meaningful occasion. In some instances, of course, a church wedding may not be feasible. The home of the bride is a good setting. Preparation and careful planning are warranted to make the event stand out with the proper significance that ought to be attached always to the linking of two lives together. Hasty and poorly planned ceremonies are not worthy of the great event in the long succession of human marriage which was first begun when the Lord God said, "It is not good for the man to be alone."

Wedding plans will, of course, be made together. It does provide a rare opportunity for the groom-to-be to display proper deference to the wishes of his bride-to-be. He will do well to let her have her way about the plans—

a practice which he will find it profitable to continue in many matters even after the ceremony.

Although the weight of responsibility is upon the pastor to bring a spiritual atmosphere into the wedding, there are things which the couple may do in that direction. The traditional songs and wedding march are so deeply engrained in our thinking of weddings that they will likely continue to be included. They do express meaningful sentiments and have real value. However, it is time for Christian young people generally to consider the inclusion of other music which is definitely Christian. For instance, "Living for Jesus" is a fine expression of firm resolve appropriate in such a setting. Another possibility is "I Would Be True." A Christian spirit in wedding plans can be cultivated by opening and closing the rehearsals with prayer. A further contribution will be made by the attitude of the participants during the moments of the ceremony. It is a time of joy to be sure, and not an occasion for giddiness or any glance of countenance which denies the holy import of the moment. The very facial expressions of the chief participants can add to or detract from the rich atmosphere which will make the moments meaningful.

3. *After You Marry*

A new home ought to be dedicated to God. Immediately after the ceremony is an appropriate time for the young couple to set their home apart unto the Lord. They will want to invite friends and neighbors to join them on this occasion. The pastor may come to assist. Here is an order which may be adapted to meet one's own needs:

Home Dedication Service

"A man shall sanctify his house to be holy unto the Lord" (Lev. 27:14).

Song: "Blest Be the Tie," by family.

Prayer Poem: "Bless This House" by Taylor.

(May be sung as solo or read)

Scripture: Psalm 127.

The Lord's Prayer: Offered in unison by group.

Husband (or leader): To Thee, O God, from whom cometh every good and perfect gift;

Wife (or both): We dedicate our home.

Husband: To the religious instruction of the children whom God gives us;

Wife: We dedicate our home.

Husband: To Christian character building through patient discipline, understanding guidance, and prayerful counsel;

Wife: We dedicate our home.

Husband: To Christian conversation, literature, art, and music;

Wife: We dedicate our home.

Husband: To choice companions, helpful hospitality, and wholesome social life;

Wife: We dedicate our home.

Husband: To personal and family worship, Bible reading, and prayer;

Wife: We dedicate our home.

Husband: To the service of Christ through his church;

Wife: We dedicate our home.

Husband: To God, our Heavenly Father, to Jesus Christ our Saviour and Lord, to the Holy Spirit our companion and comforter, whose divine presence we shall ever welcome, the unseen guest at every table and the silent listener to every conversation;

Wife: We dedicate our home.

The Dedicatory Prayer: Husband.

The genuine spirit of this dedication will be put to the test daily in your home. In the interaction of two personalities the quality of living will prove the real character of your Christianity. Gentleness, sympathy, understanding, self-control, love, exercised day by day in living relations will mark your home as manifesting the real spirit of Christ. Here in the intimate association of family life where you will be tempted to presume upon the love and the forgiveness of those who are the dearest in all of the world to you your Christianity will be tested the most severely. As its quality is proved by daily living on the high planes of tranquility and congeniality the values and meaning of a Christian home will evolve.

(1) *Three activities that will help.*—There is no simple recipe for building a Christian home. The following three activities are proposed not in any sense as a panacea, but as three practices which if followed sincerely will bring great blessings to your home.

a. Grace at meals.—The expression of thanks at mealtime has real meaning. It is a definite assertion of faith. It professes reliance upon God and thanksgiving for all of his benefits. It denies that material sustenance has come by reason of one's own cleverness, but asserts that God has done it. He has given food. He has given shelter. He has clothed and fed and sustained. Together about the table the Christian family bows in reverence and sincere gratitude. With humble petition they look to God for continued help.

Such an experience thrice a day means something to a home. It anchors the family to God. It signifies trust. It cultivates dependence. It causes the family to look to God as the source of all good things.

A little boy who was accustomed to such a practice was visiting in a home which had become careless at this point. He noticed that the father and mother and children began eating immediately without bowing their heads. Somewhat startled and confused he politely inquired if they did not return thanks before eating.

"No," said the father, "we don't take the time to do that."

God forbid that a man and his children should sit down to a table spread with material bounties from God's providential hands and not even take the time to say one word of thanksgiving!

Anyone can express thanks. He does not have to do it audibly. Any family where the responsible home builders believe that there is a God and that he has given them food can return thanks at mealtime—even if by no more than a moment of silent thanksgiving.

Christian young people who are wise will make grace at meals a definite practice in their homes.

b. Private devotions.—Every person needs some time alone each day with God. The Christian home needs to cultivate private reading of God's Word and individual prayer to God. The family by right attitudes and by provisions for privacy can make it easy for its members to grow spiritually by practicing private devotions. Let this be the spirit of your home, that the daily reading of the Bible alone in private will be cultivated persistently and continuously.

c. Family worship.—The Christian home needs the influence of a period each day of Bible reading together followed by an earnest prayer for God's blessings upon the home.

Again, this is a practice which every man and woman who believe in God, and believe that the Bible is his word, and that it will bring blessings to the family, can follow. A man can read the Book to his family. If it is no more than a single verse, he can read it, though he does it falteringly and stumblingly, still he can read the Book.

Resolve to make this significant activity the daily practice of your home. A family needs such an experience. A bride and groom need to find time to hide God's Word in their hearts together even from their wedding day. Now in these days of anticipation, make the decision that such will be the practice of your home.

III. The Sure Foundation

In conclusion, note once more the texts at the beginning of this chapter. The first points out the vanity—the utter uselessness and failure—of human effort unless the Lord is in it.

In the second passage, which concludes Jesus' great Sermon on the Mount, the obvious teaching is evident. Jesus is no doubt talking about a life. Some lives he asserts are properly founded, on the bedrock of eternal truth which is the very word of Christ. When the storms come, as certain they are to come, such lives will stand because they are well founded.

Now in each verse some proper significance may be attached to the fact that the point of the illustration centers around a house—"except the Lord build the house," "a wise man . . . built his house." A house most often is built for a residence. And a residence is the abode of a man and his wife and children—a home for those who are bound together by love. Unless the Lord is in the building of the house—in the building of the home—all efforts will fail, according to the psalmist. Unless a man founds his house—his home—on the eternal Word of God, says Jesus, his house will be swept away.

But if one's home is properly founded, when the storms come, as certain they are to come, such a home will stand. The winds of social ostracism and gossip will beat upon that house to no avail. The rains of calamity will drench it without hurt. The storms of disease, of difficulty, of death will do their worst but without hurt to such a house.

Thank God for the sure foundation, the Word of God, on which our homes may be founded with assurance that they can thereby withstand every storm that comes.

Some Things To Think About

1. What is a Christian home?
2. Formulate your platform for a Christian home.
3. Should one pray for guidance in marriage?
4. How can weddings be made to include more of the Christian spirit?
5. When should a home be dedicated?
6. Will you have family worship in your home?